新編英語

課 本

new
English
900

First Printing--------April, 1978
published by
TAIPEI PUBLICATIONS TRADING CO
P. O. Box 59326 Taipei, Taiwan
Tel: 3618722

台 灣 版

有著作權◇不准翻印

台內著字第11253號

發行人：黃　　　永　　　全
發行所：臺 北 圖 書 有 限 公 司
　　　　臺北市開封街一段六十六號407室
印刷所：文 大 印 刷 有 限 公 司
　　　　臺 北 市 萬 大 路 424 巷 16 號
新聞局出版登記局版臺業字第48號

中華民國六十七年 四 月　　日

定價 NT$

new English

book 6

Macmillan Publishing Co., Inc.
Collier Macmillan International
New York

Collier Macmillan Publishers
London

Taipei Publications Trading Co.
台北圖書有限公司

NEW ENGLISH 900

Project Editor: Peggy Intrator   **Contributing Editor:** Michael R. Lanzano

Senior Editor: Mary Ann Kingston Miller

Associate Editor: Gretchen Dowling

Consultant: Jean A. McConochie

Art Director: Zelda Haber

STAFF FOR STUDENT BOOK SIX

Editor: Marilyn G. Moller

Editorial Assistant: Elyn Raymon

Illustrator: Erica Merkling

Art Editor: Anna Sabin

Production Supervisor: Gerald Vogt

**This is a revision of English 900®,
copyright © 1964 Macmillan Publishing Co., Inc.**

Philippines Copyright © 1978 MACMILLAN PUBLISHING CO., INC.

ISBN 0-02-974430-X

Collier Macmillan International, Inc.
866 Third Avenue, New York, New York 10022
Collier Macmillan Canada, Ltd.
Collier Macmillan Publishers
London

CONTENTS

Units 43, 44, 46-49 each contain two dialogue lessons. Units 45 and 50 contain three reading lessons each. The main grammatical points featured are listed below.

Introduction

The Story So Far

INTRODUCTION

Welcome to English.

Welcome to New English 900®.

In this introduction, we want to tell you something about the books you are going to be using.

1. What is New English 900®?

NEW ENGLISH 900® is a six-level course for adult students of English as a second language. It contains material from beginning to advanced levels of study. The series consists of six student textbooks, six workbooks, six teacher's books, and reel-to-reel or cassette recordings.

2. An Updated and Revised Program

This series is a revision of the original ENGLISH 900® which takes its name from the 900 Base Sentences presented in the six textbooks. These sentences cover the basic structures and basic vocabulary of the English language. The **Base Sentences** of NEW ENGLISH 900® always appear in a complete and authentic context. They are presented in dialogue form as spoken by a cast of fully-drawn characters who use the English language in a natural way to communicate their thoughts, ideas, and feelings.

3. How Your Textbooks Are Organized

There are 150 Base Sentences in each book, and they are numbered consecutively from Base Sentence 1, Book

1, Unit 1, through Base Sentence 900 in Book 6, Unit 50. New structures are introduced in Base Sentences, and these sentences provide "building blocks" for the rest of the materials studied in the series.

a. The Dialogue Unit

There are ten units in Book 1. Each unit consists of three lessons and contains fifteen Base Sentences. In Book 1, every lesson opens with a short **Dialogue** containing the Base Sentences. As you progress through the series, a continuous and integrated story will be unfolded through the dialogues and, later, the readings. (However, each textbook can be used separately). The dialogues are followed by **Substitution Drills** that introduce variations of the Base Sentences and provide the student with the pronunciation and drill material needed for mastery. The **Exercises** in each lesson can be used as oral and written drills. In addition, every unit contains a **Grammatical Preview,** a **Refocus (review) Exercise,** and a **Bonus Dialogue.**

b. Reading and Refocus Units

Beginning with Book 2, each text contains two **Reading and Refocus Units.** These units consist of thirty Base Sentences introduced in three **Reading Passages.** They are followed by **Comprehension Questions** and **Exercises** that review and contrast aspects of the language previously introduced.

c. Intonation and Word Index

Other features of each textbook include a complete listing of the Base Sentences introduced in that book. This listing appears with **Intonation Lines.** In addition, there is a **Word Index** that lists, in alphabetical order, all the new words in the book, and notes the unit, lesson, and sentence in which each word first appeared.

4. Your Workbooks and Tapes

A companion **Workbook** is available for each of the six textbooks. The Workbooks reinforce material from the text and develop pronunciation and writing skills. They are designed to be used both at home and in the classroom.

A series of **Pre-recorded Tapes** has been prepared for language laboratory use. These tapes include all material from the Dialogues, Substitution Drills, Readings, and Comprehension Questions in the Student Books, and from the Pronunciation Exercises in the Workbooks.

5. The Teacher's Books

The **Teacher's Books** are an integral part of NEW ENGLISH 900®. Organized to correspond to the student text, the Teacher's Book offers techniques and strategies of practical value to the teacher in the classroom. Included are suggested lesson plans, cultural notes, and a step-by-step outline of ways to present and practice the new material.

Our Thanks

Based on many suggestions we have received from you, the users, we offer NEW ENGLISH 900®. It represents a careful and extensive revision of the widely popular original series. In it, we hope to have combined the best of the old with the most exciting of the new.

THE STORY SO FAR

The first five books have established the characters and plot of *New English 900*. We have met **Bill O'Neill**, an undercover policeman who sells ice cream at the World's Fair, and through him we have met **Laura Segura**, a secretary, and her ex-boss, **Mr. Crawford**. One of Mr. Crawford's sons, **Michael**, is an artist, and the other, **Gary**, left the house after a bitter argument with his father. Mr. Crawford wants Michael to join his business.

Through Bill, we met **Paulo** and **Joana Farias**. Paulo, a young businessman, is planning an art competition for the Brazilian Pavilion at the Fair. Joana, his sister, is an art student visiting from Brazil. Joana is dating Michael Crawford, and they have begun to think about marriage. Michael has decided to enter the Art Competition.

The Nikzad family is from Iran. We have met **Simon Nikzad**, a banker at the Fair, his wife, **Zahra**, and their sons, **Ali** and **Hussein**. Ali is lively, independent, and stubborn.

The O'Neill family is American. We have met Bill's wife, **Nora**, a florist, and their four children: **Billy** (Bill, Jr.), **Jack**, **Peggy**, and **Suzy**.

Miguel Morales, who has been visiting from Colombia, and **Pedro Ortega** are friends. Pedro and Miguel met the girl upstairs, **Marta Garcia**. To Pedro's surprise, Marta preferred Miguel. Marta and Miguel have continued to see each other.

Pedro, a photographer, and Michael Crawford are good friends. Because he doesn't want his father to know about it, when Michael enters the Art Competition, he uses Pedro's name.

The Yamamotos own a store near the Fair. We have met **Grandfather** and his grandson, **Jim**. We have also learned a little about **Jim's mother and father**. Through the Yamamotos, we see the changing values of three generations.

An imaginary World's Fair provides a background for the series.

UNIT 43
Good-Byes

LESSON 1

[*At the airport*]

	MARTA:	Airports are sad places.
751	MIGUEL:	Sometimes, I guess. But, we'll write. You'll come down at Christmas.751
	MARTA:	If we can find the money.
752	MIGUEL:	Don't worry, Marta. Everything will be taken care
753		of.752 They say that fares are going to be reduced in the next six months.753 And when I graduate, well . . .
	MARTA:	That's two years from now. Two years is a long time.
754	MIGUEL:	The time will pass quickly.754 You'll see. I might even
755		be able to come back to New York next summer.755

Continued

756   MARTA: Oh, Miguel, you'll forget all about me. Your mother will find you a nice girl, you'll get married, and live happily ever after.756

MIGUEL: No, I won't. I swear I won't.

[Marta shakes her head.]

MIGUEL: Don't you believe me?

757   MARTA: I don't want to talk about it. All I know is that you are going to be taken away from me.757

758   MIGUEL: That's ridiculous! I'll write every day, whether you answer me or not.758

MARTA: Don't be silly. You'll have other things to do. *[She starts to cry.]*

MIGUEL: Don't cry, Marta, please.

GRAMMATICAL PREVIEW

In Book 5, we introduced the passive voice in the present and past tenses. In the passive voice, as you know, the object of the verb becomes the subject. The old subject is frequently omitted. The verb in the passive voice is a form of BE + the past participle. Here are two more forms of the passive voice.

Transformation of the Active to the Passive Voice in the "Going To" Future Tense

Active: The airlines *are going to reduce* the fares.

Passive: Fares *are going to be reduced* (by the airlines).
           going to + BE + past participle

Transformation of the Active to the Passive Voice in the "Will" Future Tense

Active: Some woman *will take* Miguel away from Marta.

Passive: Miguel *will be taken* away from Marta (by some woman).
           will + BE + past participle

SUBSTITUTION DRILLS

1. You'll come down at Christmas.
                    *New Year's.
                    Easter.
                    Thanksgiving.

2. The time will pass   quickly.
     The days will go by
     The weeks will fly by

3. I might even be able to come back to New York next summer.
                    find a way to visit you this winter.
                    immigrate to the United States.
                    apply for a student visa.

*New Year's Day

4. I might not be able to come back to New York next summer.
    go anywhere over the Easter vacation.
    make any New Year's resolutions this year.
    have enough money to go to school next year.

5. You'll get married and live happily ever after.
    for the rest of your life.
    forever.
    until the end of time!

6. Marta doesn't know whether she'll be able to go to Bogotá at
    Christmas.
    if   Miguel will wait for her.
    she will ever see Miguel again.
    Miguel's parents will approve of her

7. All I know   is that you are going to be taken
    away from me.
The only thing I'm sure about
The only important thing
All that's important
The only thing I know

CONNECTED DRILLS

1. Do you think you'll   come back next summer?
    Miguel will
    Mrs. Farias will
    Arturo and Miguel will
    we'll

—I   might.
He
She
They
We

---

2. I'll write to you every day   **whether** you answer me   or not.
I swear it's true   you believe me
Miguel has to go home   he likes it
My sister is going to college   she gets a scholarship
Pedro will always chase women   he gets married

3. I'll write to you every day   **whether or not** you answer.
I swear it's true   you believe me.
Miguel has to go home   he likes the idea.
My sister is going to college   she wins a
                                                                        scholarship.
Pedro will always chase women   he gets married.

4. a. They say the fares are going to be reduced.
                    the article isn't going to be published.
                    our salaries will be increased.
                    the thief will never be caught.
                    Smith is going to be elected.

b. They say the airlines are going to reduce the fares.
                    paper isn't going to publish the article.
                    company is going to increase our salaries.
                    police will never catch the thief.
                    people are going to elect Smith.

5. a. All I know is that you are going to be taken away from me.
                    the fares aren't going to be reduced.
                    the exam is going to be given soon.
                    I'm not going to be met at the airport.

b. All I know is that someone is going to take you away from
                    me.
                    the airlines aren't going to reduce the fares.
                    the professor is going to give the exam soon.
                    no one is going to meet me at the airport.

EXERCISES

1. Change these sentences with "even if" to two sentences with "whether or not."

Example: Miguel will find time to write to Marta even if he's busy.
1. *Miguel will find time to write to Marta whether or not he's busy.*
2. *Miguel will find time to write to Marta whether he's busy or not.*

a.   I'm going to take the expressway even if the traffic is heavy.
b.   Jack takes the dog for a walk even if it's raining.
c.   Joana hopes Michael will continue to paint even if he doesn't win the competition.
d.   I can study even if the radio is on.
e.   Mrs. Farias is planning to stay in Brazil even if her children stay in New York.
f.   Ali has to start school this fall even if he doesn't like the idea.

2. Change the sentences as in the examples. Use "might" or "might not."

Examples: 1. It's possible that the restaurant is open on Mondays.
The restaurant might be open on Mondays.

2. It's possible that Miguel will forget about Marta.
Miguel might forget about Marta.

3. It's possible that I have change for a ten-dollar bill.
I might have change for a ten-dollar bill.

4. It's possible Marta won't be able to go to Bogotá at Christmas.
Marta might not be able to go to Bogotá at Christmas.

a.   It's possible that the phone is out of order.
b.   It's possible that Miguel will immigrate to the United States.

c. It's possible that the restaurant has a terrace.
d. It's possible that we won't go anywhere this weekend.
e. It's possible that Paulo isn't at the office today.
f. It's possible that you have the flu.
g. It's possible that we will see Miguel off at the airport.
h. It's possible that those people are lost.

3. Use the *will* future passive form of the verb in these sentences.

Examples: 1. I'm sure the money _____ somewhere. (*find*)
   I'm sure the money will be found somewhere.

   2. _____ Michael _____ to the party?
   (*invite*)
   Will Michael be invited to the party?

a. The flight _____ because of the bad weather. (*cancel*)
b. _____ Paulo _____ to make a speech at the ceremony? (*ask*)
c. The old train station _____ as a restaurant. (*use*)
d. Beethoven's Fifth Symphony _____ by the World's Fair Orchestra. (*perform*)
e. The President _____ at the station by the Mayor and other important people. (*greet*)

4. Answer the questions using the *going to* future passive form.

Example: When is the mailman going to pick up the mail? (*at 11 o'clock*)
   The mail is going to be picked up at 11 o'clock.

a. When are they going to complete the new gymnasium? (*in July*)
b. Where is the Brazilian Pavilion going to exhibit the paintings? (*at the World's Fair Museum of Modern Art*)
c. When is the History Department going to give the exam? (*in two weeks*)
d. What is the company going to spend the money on? (*a new office building*)
e. When are they going to return the books? (*on Monday*)

LESSON 2

759	MIGUEL:	Look, here come Mrs. Ortega and Pedro.
	MARTA:	I wish they would go away.
	MIGUEL:	You don't really mean that, Marta.
760	PEDRO:	[*Pedro clears his throat.*] I hope we're not interrupting anything.₇₆₀ We want to say good-bye, too.
761	MRS. ORTEGA:	Let me give you a kiss, my boy.₇₆₁
762		Remember me to your mother and
763		father.₇₆₂ I hope to see them again.₇₆₃ I'll miss you, Miguel.
	MIGUEL:	I'll miss you, too. It's been a wonderful summer. Thank you. Take care of Pedro. He still needs his mama.
	PEDRO:	[*smiling*] Good-bye, kid. [*They shake hands.*]
	LOUDSPEAKER:	Last call for Flight 629 for Bogotá, leaving from Gate 10.

764 MARTA: You'd better hurry, Miguel.₇₆₄ [*She turns away.*]

  MIGUEL: Don't cry, Marta.

765 SECURITY OFFICER: [*to Marta*] Sorry, Miss. Only passengers are allowed beyond this point.₇₆₅

  MIGUEL: Marta? . . . [*Miguel turns away and runs toward the gate.*]

  MARTA: Good-bye, Miguel. [*He turns and waves.*]

SUBSTITUTION DRILLS

1. Look, here come Mrs. Ortega and Pedro.
       here comes the bus.
       there go Miguel and Marta.
       there goes the mailman.

2. Let me give you a kiss,   **my boy.**
       shake your hand,
       kiss you good-bye,
       give you some advice,
       give you a going-away present,

3. Remember me   to your mother and father.
Give my regards
Give my love

4. I wish they would go away.
       you weren't leaving.
       she wouldn't cry.
       Miguel could stay in New York.
       they would leave us alone.

5. I hope we're not interrupting anything.
       we're not disturbing anyone.
       Miguel will be happy back in Colombia.
       Marta isn't going to cry.
       I'm not keeping you from something.

6. I hope to see them again.
       come back next summer.
       return one day.
       hear from Miguel soon.
       pay the Ortegas a visit in the spring.

7. You   had **better hurry.**
 I   'd
 We
 Miguel
 He
 Miguel and Marta
 They

8. You'd better hurry.
          watch the time.
          check your luggage.
          get some sleep.
          stop smoking.

9. You'd better not forget to write.
          take too much luggage.
          disturb Miguel and Marta.
          unfasten your seat belt.
          be late.

10. Only passengers are allowed beyond this point.
          past the gate.
          through the security check.
          in the duty-free shops.
          on the airplane.

EXERCISES

1. Give advice using "had better" or "had better not."

Examples: 1. Miguel hasn't slept well all week. (*he/try to get some rest*)
He'd better try to get some rest.

2. The sky is gray and cloudy. (*you/not forget your umbrella*)
You'd better not forget your umbrella.

a. There are two sections in the plane, smoking and no smoking. Miguel can't stand cigarette smoke. (*he/sit in the no smoking section*)
b. Miguel and Marta look as if they're having a private conversation. (*we/not disturb them*)
c. It's eight p.m. Everyone is having coffee and dessert, but coffee keeps Joana awake. (*she/not have any coffee*)
d. There's someone at the door. (*I/see who it is*)
e. Ali and Hussein are at a neighbor's pool. They don't know how to swim very well. (*they/not go into deep water*)
f. Miguel's plane is leaving in ten minutes. He hasn't checked his luggage yet. (*he/hurry up*)
g. I didn't bring anything to read on the plane. I will be bored if I have nothing to read. (*you/buy a magazine*)

2. Change the sentences.

Example: Mrs. Ortega hopes **she will** see Miguel's parents again.
Mrs. Ortega hopes to see Miguel's parents again.

a. Miguel hopes he will find time to write to Marta every day.
b. Michael hopes he will win the competition.
c. Mrs. Farias hopes she will see her children again soon.
d. I hope I'll be able to go to Bogotá at Christmas.
e. Marta and Miguel hope they will be able to visit each other next year.

3. Make one sentence.

Example: Will Miguel come back to New York next summer?
Marta hopes he will.
Marta hopes Miguel will come back to New York next
summer.

a. Will Michael win the competition? Joana hopes he will.
b. Will Marta cry at the airport? Miguel hopes she won't.
c. Will Ali behave in school next year? Mrs. Nikzad hopes he will.
d. Will Miguel have a good flight? Mrs. Ortega hopes he will.
e. Will Paulo and Joana stay in New York City? Mrs. Farias hopes
they won't.

4. Use *hope, hopes, wish,* or *wishes* in the sentences below.

Examples: 1. I _____ it doesn't rain tomorrow. We're
planning on going to the beach.
I hope it doesn't rain tomorrow.

2. Claire _____ she had more time to read, but
she's very busy these days.
*Claire wishes she had more time to read, but she's
very busy these days.*

a. I _____ I knew what to get Miguel for a going-away
present. I've looked in all the department stores, but I can't
seem to find just the right thing.
b. Miguel _____ he can get a window seat on the plane.
He likes to watch the plane take off and land.
c. Henry's wife _____ he would quit smoking. He smokes
three packs a day, and she's worried about his health.

d. I _____ I'm not keeping you from something. I just stopped in to say hello.

e. Miguel _____ he hasn't left anything behind. He packed in such a hurry.

f. Claire _____ the banks didn't close at three o'clock. She works until five, and she can never get there on her lunch hour.

g. Michael _____ he won't have to go into business with his father. He'd rather be a painter.

h. I _____ Miguel has room for everything in his suitcase. He bought a lot of gifts to take back to Colombia.

i. Marta _____ Pedro and Mrs. Ortega would go away. She doesn't want them to see her crying.

j. Jack _____ the teacher isn't going to give a surprise test this afternoon. He didn't do his homework last night.

k. Miguel _____ Marta could come with him to Bogotá. Unfortunately, she has to stay in New York.

l. Joana and Paulo _____ they'll receive a letter from their mother soon. It's been a week since she left New York, and they still haven't heard from her.

UNIT 44
Only Five More Days

LESSON 1

	ALI:	How many days to my birthday?
	MRS. NIKZAD:	Five.
	ALI:	Are we going to invite Mr. Yamamoto, the vegetable man, to my party?
766 767	MRS. NIKZAD:	I don't think so, dear. We don't know him very well, and he might be too busy to come. 766 I understand his store is being renovated next week. 767
768	ALI:	Oh. And what about Mr. O'Neill? Is he coming?
768	MRS. NIKZAD:	He's been invited.
	ALI:	But is he coming?
	MRS. NIKZAD:	We haven't heard from him yet, Ali.
	ALI:	I hope he comes.
769	MRS. NIKZAD:	Don't worry, Ali. I'm sure he'll try his best. 769
	ALI:	What about Mr. Yamamoto?
	MRS. NIKZAD:	I don't know, dear.
	ALI:	But I want to invite him.
	MRS. NIKZAD:	Let's wait and ask your father.
	ALI:	Do we have to wait?
770	MRS. NIKZAD:	Of course, Ali. But don't be upset. The invitation can be sent out first thing in the morning. 770
771	ALI:	I'm going outside. 771 O.K.?
772	MRS. NIKZAD:	All right, dear. Don't be too long. 772 It's almost lunch time. [Ali leaves.]

GRAMMATICAL PREVIEW

Transformation of the Active to the Passive Voice in the Present Perfect Tense

Active:	The Nikzads *have taken* Ali around the world a few times.
Passive:	Ali *has been taken* around the world (by the Nikzads) a few times.

Just as in the active voice, the present perfect passive indicates that at some indefinite time in the past, events occurred whose effects are still being felt.

Transformation of the Active to the Passive with Modals

Active:	We *can send out* the invitation in the morning.
Passive:	The invitation *can be sent out* (by us) in the morning.

Transformation of the Active to the Passive Voice in the Present Continuous Tense

Active:	The workmen *are renovating* Mr. Yamamoto's store.
Passive:	Mr. Yamamoto's store *is being renovated* (by the workmen).

Just as in the active voice, the present continuous passive indicates an action that is going on now. It may have started in the past, and it might continue for awhile, but it is definitely a current activity.

SUBSTITUTION DRILLS

1. We don't know him very well,
        and he might **be too busy to come.**
                                    be visiting relatives that day.
                                    have other plans.
                                    not be able to get away from the store.
                                    not want to come to a children's party.

2. He's been **invited to the party.**
                    advised to wait.
                    offered a very good job.
                    encouraged to come.

3. He   **might be too busy to come.**
    Mrs. O'Neill
    I
    We
    The Crawfords

4. He may not **have time to come.**
                    reply to our invitation.
                    be able to take Monday off.
                    feel comfortable with strangers.
                    have a way to get to the party.

5. I'm sure he'll **try his best**   **to come.**
                    do his best
                    do everything in his power
                    make time

6. The invitation **can**   **be sent out first thing in the morning.**
                    should
                    ought to
                    has to
                    will

7. The invitation can be sent out first thing in the morning.
                            delivered
                            mailed
                            answered

8. I'm going out.
                 outside.
                 outdoors.
                 out for a minute.
                 out to play.

9. Don't be too long.
          be away
          be gone
          stay outside

CONNECTED DRILLS

1. I understand his store is being renovated next week.
                  Ali   given a new bike.
                  the ice cream   ordered in advance.
                  the party   held in an ice cream parlor.
                  the bill   paid in advance.

2. All the neighbors   are being invited to Ali's party.
Some of Ali's classmates   invited, too.
The invitations   sent out tomorrow morning.
The presents   bought this week.
The reservations   made well in advance.

3. The Yamamotos   haven't been invited to the party yet.
The reservations   confirmed
All the arrangements   made
Some of the presents   bought
Ali's classmates   invited

EXERCISES

1. Use "may" or "may not" in the sentences.

Examples: 1. **Maybe** Mr. Yamamoto **will** be too busy to come to
Ali's party.
*Mr. Yamamoto may be too busy to come to Ali's
party.*

2. **Maybe** Mr. Yamamoto **won't** have time to come to
Ali's party.
*Mr. Yamamoto may not have time to come to Ali's
party.*

a. Maybe Ali will get a stomachache if he eats too much ice
cream.
b. Maybe Jack will become a policeman when he graduates from
high school.
c. Maybe Mr. Nikzad won't be able to come home for dinner
tonight.
d. Maybe there won't be enough time to notify everyone of the
change in plans.
e. Maybe the brochures for the art competition won't be ready in
time.

Rewrite the following sentences in the passive voice. Omit the agent.

Examples: 1. The university is scheduling several new courses for next semester.
Several new courses are being scheduled for next semester.

2. Are the garage attendants servicing your car?
Is your car being serviced?

a. The bank is giving a free gift to each new customer.
b. Are they paving the road in front of your house?
c. They are announcing the winner of the art competition on New Year's Day.

d. The Nikzads aren't inviting Hussein's friends to Ali's birthday party.
e. Is an undercover policeman following the suspects?
f. The department store isn't putting pocket calculators on sale until after the first of the year.

3. Rewrite the following sentences in the passive voice. Omit the agent.

Examples: 1. Someone has eaten all of the cake.
All of the cake has been eaten.

2. No one has invited him to Ali's party.
He hasn't been invited to Ali's party.

3. Has anyone ever robbed Mr. Yamamoto's store?
Has Mr. Yamamoto's store ever been robbed?

a. Someone has asked me to join the English Conversation Club.
b. No one has washed the dishes.
c. Has anyone ever invited you to a surprise birthday party? `
d. No one has rented the apartment next to mine yet.
e. Has anyone fixed that machine yet?
f. Someone has taken out the garbage.

LESSON 2

[One and a half hours later Mrs. Nikzad is on the phone with her husband.]

	MRS. NIKZAD:	Hello, Simon. Have you seen Ali this afternoon?
	MR. NIKZAD:	No, Zahra. Why?
773	MRS. NIKZAD:	Oh, dear. I can't find him anywhere. I thought
774		he might have gone to the Fair.773 I've looked
775		all over.774 I don't know what to do. He
		should have been back an hour ago.775
	MR. NIKZAD:	Don't worry, Zahra. Probably, he's visiting a
		friend and forgot about the time.
776	MRS. NIKZAD:	But an hour and a half? That's not like him. He
		could have had an accident.776
777	MR. NIKZAD:	Yes, he could have, Zahra, but he probably
		didn't.777 Did anything happen this morning?
		What were you talking about before he left?
	MRS. NIKZAD:	His birthday party. It's all he talks about lately.
	MR. NIKZAD:	Is it possible you said something to upset him?

778 MRS. NIKZAD: I must have.₇₇₈ I know he was upset because we
                   haven't received Mr. O'Neill's reply to our
                   invitation, and . . .

     MR. NIKZAD: And?

     MRS. NIKZAD: And because we haven't invited Mr. Yamamoto.

     MR. NIKZAD: Anything else?

779 MRS. NIKZAD: No. He left the house right after that. I suppose I
                   should have called you earlier.₇₇₉

     MR. NIKZAD: Zahra, I'm sure there's nothing to worry about.
                   He's probably on his way to the Fair to see
                   Mr. O'Neill, or else he's with Mr. Yamamoto.

     MRS. NIKZAD: Oh, wait! Here he is! And Mr. Yamamoto is with
780   him. You were right, Simon. He must have
                   gone to Mr. Yamamoto's.₇₈₀

GRAMMATICAL PREVIEW

Modals with the Present Perfect Tense

When we use a modal with the present perfect tense, we follow the form below.

	MODALS	HAVE	PAST PARTICIPLE	
Miguel	could should might may ought to must can't	have	stayed	in New York.

The meaning of such sentences comes from a combination of the modal and the present perfect verb.

SUBSTITUTION DRILLS

1. Do you know where Ali is? I haven't seen him all afternoon.
   —He might have gone to the Fair.
   the park.
   a friend's house.
   see Mr. O'Neill.
   Mr. Yamamoto's store.

2. I've looked all over.
   looked everywhere.
   searched high and low.
   checked all the usual places.
   searched the whole neighborhood.

3. What do you think could have happened to him?
—He could have **had an accident.**
    hurt himself.
    gotten lost.
    forgotten about the time.
    spent his money on ice cream.

4. He **could** have had an accident, but probably he didn't.
    might
    may

5. I suppose I should have **called you earlier.**
    taken an umbrella.
    closed the windows.
    bought more bread.
    cashed a check.

CONNECTED DRILLS

1. **Mr. Nikzad didn't see Ali this afternoon.**
    Ali couldn't read the sign.
    Miguel didn't buy many things to take to Colombia.
    Marta hasn't received a letter from Miguel.

        He must not have been home.
                learned to read yet.
                had enough money.
                written to her.

2. **Could Ali have gone to Mr. Yamamoto's?** —**Yes, he could   have.**
    Did you offend her?   —I think I might
    Should we have made an appointment? —Yes, you should
    Did you say anything to upset him?   —I guess I might

3. He couldn't have **gotten lost.**
    been at Jimmy's.
    left school.
    gone to the bank.
    received our invitation yet.

   He knows his way around.
   Jimmy and his family are away on vacation.
   It's two o'clock and school isn't over until three.
   The bank is closed this afternoon.
   We only sent the invitations out this morning.

4. Ali **isn't home yet.**
    didn't say where he was going.
    didn't pick up his toys.
    didn't excuse himself from the dinner table.
    almost got hit by a car.

   He should have been back hours ago.
              told you where he was going.
              picked them up.
              excused himself.
              been more careful crossing the street.

5. Ali **went to the Fair alone.**
    upset his mother.
    punched Jimmy in the nose.
    got a stomachache from eating too much ice cream.

   He shouldn't have gone there by himself.
              worried her.
              done that.
              eaten so much ice cream.

6. Ali likes to talk to Mr. Yamamoto.
apologized to his mother.
fell asleep right after dinner.
lost his jacket.

He **must have** gone to Mr. Yamamoto's.
known she was upset.
been exhausted.
left it on the bus.

EXERCISES

1. Use "might have" or "might not have" in the sentences.

Examples: 1. It's possible that Ali got lost.
Ali might have gotten lost.

2. It's possible that Ali didn't go to Mr. Yamamoto's.
Ali might not have gone to Mr. Yamamoto's.

a. It's possible that Mrs. Nikzad upset Ali.
b. It's possible that they didn't receive your letter.
c. It's possible that he left work early.
d. It's possible that the mailman hasn't come yet.
e. It's possible that Paulo was delayed at the office.
f. It's possible that the door wasn't locked.

2. Use "could have" or "couldn't have" (past ability) in each of the blanks below.

Examples: 1. I was hungry and _____ (eat) a big breakfast, but there wasn't any food in the house.
I was hungry and <u>could have eaten</u> a big breakfast, but there wasn't any food in the house.

2. The baby _____ (break) the window.
   He can't reach that high.
   The baby <u>*couldn't have broken*</u> *the window.*
   He can't reach that high.

a. I _____ (study) for the exam, but I didn't want to.
b. Michael didn't go to college even though he _____.
c. He _____ (rob) the bank because he <u>was</u> on the other
    side of town when the robbery was taking place.
d. Joana was very excited about the art competition. As a matter
    of fact, she _____ (be) more excited.
e. We were lost in the mountains, and _____ (find) our
    way out without the help of the old fur trapper. We owe our
    lives to him.

3. Make sentences with "should have" or "shouldn't have" as in the examples.

Examples: 1. As Ali crossed the street, he almost got hit by a car.
(*be more careful*)
He should have been more careful.

2. Michael didn't get much sleep last night. (*stay up so late*)
He shouldn't have stayed up so late.

a.   Jack and Billy got in trouble. (*start a fight in the schoolyard*)
b.   I was bored on the long flight. (*forget to bring a book with me*)
c.   When he fell out of the tree, Ali broke his arm. (*try to eat ice cream and climb trees at the same time*)
d.   We couldn't get tickets to the game. (*buy them earlier*)

4. Make sentences with "must have" or "must not have" as in the examples.

Examples: 1. On the way home from the Fair, Ali lost his jacket.
(*leave it on the bus*)
He must have left it on the bus.

2. Marta wasn't at the English Conversation Club meeting. (*remember it*)
She must not have remembered it.

a.   Jack has a black eye. (*be in a fight*)
b.   Pedro met an old friend on the street and couldn't remember her name. (*be embarrassed*)
c.   By mistake, Mr. Crawford went through a red light. (*see it*)
d.   Laura had a headache and a sore throat. (*catch a cold*)
e.   The Crawfords had to wait an hour for a table at the new French restaurant. (*make a reservation*)
f.   Joana and Michael saw the movie three times. (*enjoy it very much*)
g.   The "Apartment for Rent" sign was still on the front door this morning. (*be rented yet*)

UNIT 45
Reading and Refocus

LESSON 1

Ali Found

781 MRS. NIKZAD: Ali, my little Martian. Where were you? Why
didn't you tell me where you were go-
782 ing?₇₈₁ You've been gone three hours! Mr.
Yamamoto, I can't thank you enough for
bringing him back.₇₈₂ [*She starts crying.*]
What happened, Ali? Where were you? I
was so worried.

ALI: Don't cry, Mommy. I won't do it again. I
promise. Don't cry. I just went to Mr.
Yamamoto's store to invite him to my
783 party. It takes too long to invite people by
784 mail.₇₈₃ I got lost. I started walking, and
785 then I didn't know where I was.₇₈₄ So I
asked people to help me find Mr.
786 Yamamoto's store.₇₈₅ Some people said,
"Turn left," and some people said, "Turn
right," and sometimes I forgot what they
said.₇₈₆ But *I* didn't get scared! I kept
saying to myself, "You're almost seven!"
787 Anyway, all of a sudden, I was right there
788 in front of Mr. Yamamoto's store.₇₈₇ It was
like magic!₇₈₈ And Mr. Yamamoto can
come to my party. I asked him.

789 MR. YAMAMOTO: You should have seen him, Mrs. Nikzad.₇₈₉
790 When Ali found the store, he may have
been shaking a little, but he wouldn't
cry.₇₉₀ He's a brave boy.

Questions about "Ali Found"

Fact:
The answers are *clear* in the story.
1. Did Ali tell his mother where he was going?
2. How long was Ali gone?
3. Did Ali go to Mr. Yamamoto's store to buy some fruit or to invite him to the birthday party?
4. Did Ali succeed in what he wanted to do?
5. When he finally got to Mr. Yamamoto's store, was Ali shaking because he was scared or because he was cold?
6. How did Mrs. Nikzad feel when she saw that Ali was safe with Mr. Yamamoto?

Inference:
You can *guess the right answers* from the story.
1. Why did Ali say, "Don't cry, Mommy"?
2. Who was more upset, Mrs. Nikzad or Ali?
3. Why did Ali keep saying to himself, "You're almost seven"?
4. Did Ali think he could find Mr. Yamamoto's store by himself when he left the apartment?
5. Did the people whom Ali asked give him good directions to Mr. Yamamoto's store?
6. Why wouldn't Ali cry?

To the Student:
There are *no wrong answers* to these questions.
1. What do you think about Ali's behavior when he realized he was lost?
2. In your opinion, should Mrs. Nikzad have scolded Ali more when Mr. Yamamoto brought him home?
3. Do you think Ali will keep his promise to his mother or not?
4. Do you admire Ali's independent nature or not?
5. Would you like to have a son or a little brother like Ali?
6. Why do you think Mr. Yamamoto likes Ali?

USING YOUR ENGLISH

MODALS—with Passive Voice and Perfect Tense(s)

The same modal auxiliary verb can often be used to express several
different meanings. In the chart below you can find some of the
most common modals and their meanings.

PERMISSION	POSSIBILITY	ABILITY	VALUE JUDGMENT
may can	may might could can	can could	should ought to have to could

PROBABILITY or EXPECTATION	NECESSITY or OBLIGATION	LOGICAL INFERENCE	WARNING or ADVICE
should ought to have to	must have to (ought to) (should)	must must have —(ed)	had better should· ought to

Note: One use of the modal *could* is as the past of *can.*
　　　One use of the modal *might* is as the past of *may.* However,
　　　when you are talking about possibilities, in the present or
　　　future tenses, you can use either *may* or *might. May* is a little
　　　more formal.

A. The following sentences are in the passive voice and use modals. Choose the most suitable meaning for each sentence. Circle the letter of your choice.

1. The grammar in John's composition *could be improved.*
   a. It's a good idea to improve the grammar.
   b. It's possible to improve the grammar.
   c. It's necessary to improve the grammar.
   d. John has the ability to improve the grammar.

2. The grammar in John's composition *ought to be improved.*
   a. It would be a good idea to improve the grammar.
   b. It's possible to improve the grammar.
   c. It's necessary to improve the grammar.
   d. John has the ability to improve the grammar.

3. The grammar in John's composition *must be improved.*
   a. It's a good idea to improve the grammar.
   b. It's possible to improve the grammar.
   c. It's necessary to improve the grammar.
   d. John has the ability to improve the grammar.

4. John *could be taught* better grammar. He is intelligent, but he doesn't pay attention.
   a. It's a good idea to improve his grammar.
   b. It's possible to improve his grammar.
   c. It's necessary to improve his grammar.
   d. John has the ability to improve his grammar.

5. The invitation *can be sent out* first thing in the morning.
   a. Mr. Nikzad has permission to send out the invitation first thing in the morning.
   b. Ali has permission to send out the invitation first thing in the morning.
   c. It is possible and all right to send out the invitation first thing in the morning.
   d. It is possible and all right to send Ali out first thing in the morning.

6. Ali *must have been upset* by something.
   a. It is logical to think that something upset Ali.
   b. It was Ali's duty to get upset by something.
   c. Ali probably had an upset stomach because he ate too much ice cream.
   d. It's a good thing Ali had an upset stomach because he ate too much ice cream.

7. The problem *might be discussed* at the meeting, if there is enough time.
   a. We were told to discuss the problem if there was enough time.
   b. It was possible that the problem was discussed.
   c. It is possible that the problem will be discussed.
   d. It is a good idea to discuss the problem if there is enough time.

8. The job *must be finished* by Friday, no matter what.
   a. It's logical to think that the job will be finished by Friday.
   b. We have to do the job by Friday.
   c. It's possible that the job will be done by Friday.
   d. It's a good idea to get the job done by Friday.

9. The job *must be finished* by now. John's been working on it all week.
   a. It was John's obligation to finish the job yesterday.
   b. It's logical to think that the job is completed.
   c. It's possible that the job has been finished by now.
   d. It's a good idea to finish the job now.

10. The new exhibition *has to be seen* to *be believed.*
    a. It's an obligation to see the exhibition, in order to believe how beautiful it is.
    b. It's logical to see the exhibition, in order to believe how beautiful it is.
    c. It's necessary to see the exhibition, in order to believe how beautiful it is.
    d. It's a good idea to see the exhibition, in order to see how beautiful it is.

B. The following sentences are in the active voice, in the present perfect tense. Insert one of the following modals in each blank. Most of the time, more than one answer is possible. It depends on the meaning you want to express. Use each modal at least once.

could	*had better*	*should*	*may*
must	*have (has) to*	*ought to*	*might*

1. Ali _____ have gone to the Fair. That's one possibility.

2. Bill _____ have been home hours ago. I expected him at 5:00, but it's already 8:00, and he's not here.

3. You _____ have done that job perfectly before you show it to Mr. Crawford. I warn you, he's in a terrible mood!

4. Something _____ have upset him. That's the only logical reason for his behavior.

5. I'm sorry I'm late. I guess I _____have called you before.
   —Yes, you _____ have. And you _____ have, too. You certainly had a dime for the phone.

6. Claire _____n't have typed that letter! *She* doesn't make so many mistakes.

7. Laura _____ have gone to her interview on time. She lost a good job by being late.

8. You _____ have seen the movie with us. It was wonderful!

9. Have you ever met Dr. Smith?
   —I think I _____ have. The name is familiar, though I can't remember what he looks like.

10. That man _____ have been the thief. His fingerprints are all over the safe.

11. Ali _____n't have gone to Mr. Yamamoto's without telling his mother first.

LESSON 2

It's Not the Same

Dear Pedro,

791   I've been back over a week now.
792   I expected to have trouble adjusting to life in New York, but no one ever told me that I would have trouble
793   readjusting to my old life!₇₉₂ I don't understand it. I get angry at things that never used to get me angry.₇₉₃ I lose patience
794   with my family. And unless I calm down, I'm going to lose
795   my friends, too.₇₉₄ I must have changed.₇₉₅ Everybody says I have. I know I see the world differently now, but I don't want to be the person I was before I went away. What do I do now, Pedro?
796   I miss Marta every minute, but I won't say any more about that because I can just hear you making fun of me.₇₉₆ I even
797   miss you! Which reminds me, how did your interview go?₇₉₇
798   Did you get the assistant manager position?₇₉₈
   You know, Pedro, there is no way I can repay the kindness that you and your family have shown me. All I can say is thank you, and I hope that someday soon you will visit us. Our house is your house.

Miguel

799   P.S. I know you don't write letters, but you could send a postcard every now and then.₇₉₉
800   P.P.S. I must have been in a daze when I left New York.₈₀₀ You know my sweater, the one you always used to bórrow? I must have left it at your apartment. If you find it, keep it for me until I return. It looks good on you.

Questions about "It's Not the Same"

Fact:
The answers are *clear* in the letter.
1. Has Miguel been back home for a week or more than a week?
2. Is Miguel finding it easy to readjust to life in his own country?
3. Of all the people Miguel met in New York, whom does he miss the most?
4. What kind of position is Pedro applying for?
5. Did living in New York change Miguel?
6. Is Pedro a person who writes to his friends a lot?

Inference:
You can *guess the right* answers from the letter.
1. Doesn't Pedro have time to write to Miguel?
2. What surprises Miguel most about his return to Colombia?
3. Was Miguel really bothered by Pedro's teasing, or was he just teasing Pedro back?
4. Is Miguel really surprised that he misses Pedro?
5. How does Miguel feel about the way the Ortegas treated him?
6. If Pedro ever goes to Bogotá, will he have to stay at a hotel?

To the Student:
There are *no wrong answers* to these questions.
1. Do you think Marta and Miguel will grow apart or remain in love with each other?
2. Do you suppose part of Miguel's difficulty readjusting comes from the fact that he has grown apart from his family and friends?
3. Do you think Pedro will write a letter back to Miguel, send him a postcard, or not write at all?
4. Have you ever had a readjustment experience similar to Miguel's?
5. What do you think is the hardest thing for Miguel to get used to again at home?
6. What advice would you give Miguel about readjusting to living at home again?

USING YOUR ENGLISH

I. THE PASSIVE VOICE with AGENTS

A. As you know, the agent is often omitted in passive voice sentences.

Example: *Dinner is served from 6:00 to 11:00.*
(The agent, in this case, the waiter, is omitted because the speaker doesn't care who is serving.)

1. The Personal Agent:
The personal agent is expressed when you want to emphasize or clarify *who* did the action.

Examples: 1. *Dinner was served by the management of the restaurant during the waiters' strike.*
2. *New English 900 is published by Macmillan Publishing Co., Inc.*

2. The Impersonal Agent:
Some agents are not people or groups of people. They are things such as objects, actions, facts, or qualities. These agents are not omitted.

Examples: 1. *Most people are annoyed by rudeness.*
2. *Mr. Crawford was displeased by Laura's resignation.*

B. The following sentences are in the active voice. They express ideas that, in the passive voice, need the agent included. Change them to the passive, with the agent.

Example: Ali's absence worried Mrs. Nikzad.
Mrs. Nikzad was worried by Ali's absence.

1. Ali's bravery impressed Mr. Yamamoto.
2. The change in culture confuses Miguel.
3. Ali's invitation pleased Bill.
4. Pedro and Mrs. Ortega interrupted Marta and Miguel.

5. The possibility that Miguel might marry Marta troubles Miguel's mother.
6. Pedro's teasing embarrasses Miguel.
7. The Ice Cream Company doesn't employ Bill; the Police Department employs him as an undercover agent.
8. The noise and laughter at Ali's birthday party delighted the people who passed the Ice Cream Parlor.
9. Shakespeare wrote *Romeo and Juliet.*
10. Mr. Yamamoto respects Ali, his mother cares for him, his father disciplines him, Bill feeds him, and all four love him.

II. THE PASSIVE VOICE has all the tenses that active voice verbs have.

A. For example:

PAST	PAST CONTINUOUS	PRESENT PERFECT	PRESENT
was ⎱ —*ed were ⎰	was ⎱ being — ed were ⎰ was ⎱ going to be — ed were ⎰	has ⎱ been — ed have ⎰	am ⎱ is ⎱ — ed are ⎰

PRESENT CONTINUOUS	FUTURE	FUTURE PERFECT
am is being ⎱ — ed are ⎰	will be ⎱ — ed am ⎰ is going to be ⎱ — ed are ⎰	will have been ⎱ — ed

*"—ed", here, stands for the past participle.

B. In the exercise below, fill in the blanks with the most suitable of the
following tense clues. Use each one once.

already
While
as soon as Ali
  can do it
	but now he is
	yet
	before anyone else
	during the next few
	  days
		usually
		By the time the party
		  is over
		still

1. Mr. O'Neill has _____ been invited to the party.
2. He was asked _____.
3. Several more guests are _____ being contacted.
4. They will be called _____.
5. Who hasn't been invited _____?
6. Mr. Yamamoto hasn't been asked yet, but he will be

   _____.
7. At first, he wasn't going to be invited, _____.
8. Adults aren't _____ invited to a child's party, but Ali's
   an unusual person.
9. _____ the guest list was being drawn up, Ali
   seemed nervous.
10. _____, a lot of ice cream will have been eaten.

LESSON 3

Art Competition Brochure

801   Attention young artists!

802   The Brazilian Pavilion of the World's Fair is sponsoring an international art competition. The winner will receive a $10,000 a year grant to live and study for two years at the

803   institution of his choice anywhere in Brazil. 802 All men and women under thirty years of age are cordially invited to enter the competition. 803

804   During December we will be exhibiting as many entries as

805   possible at the World's Fair Museum of Modern Art. 804 But, as the judges, all internationally famous artists, must make their decision before January 1, the Brazilian Pavilion must receive your entry by December 1. 805

806   On January 1 the Brazilian Pavilion will have the pleasure

807   of announcing the results of the competition. 806 The ceremony will take place in the Grand Gallery of the Museum at 4:30 p.m. 807

808   All works of art remain your property and will be returned

809   after the first of the year. 808 As we cannot be liable for paintings submitted to us, please insure your entry against loss, damage, or destruction. 809

810   Persons related to the staff of the Brazilian Pavilion are not eligible to enter the competition. 810

Questions about "Art Competition"

Fact:
The answers are *clear* in the brochure.
1. What kind of competition is the Brazilian Pavilion sponsoring?
2. Will the winner receive a two-year or a three-year scholarship?
3. Can anyone enter the contest?
4. Will the Pavilion keep the paintings or will it return them?
5. Will the Pavilion exhibit all the paintings it receives?
6. Where will the Pavilion announce the results of the competition?

Inference:
You can *guess the right answers* from the brochure.
1. Is the competition more for established artists or for aspiring artists?
2. Could the winner of the competition study art in Paris?
3. Will the Pavilion accept a painting that arrives on December 2?
4. Can Joana enter the competition?
5. How could the paintings be lost, damaged, or destroyed?
6. How long will the Pavilion exhibit the paintings?

To the Student:
There are *no wrong answers* to these questions.
1. Are you interested in art?
2. Would you prefer to see an exhibition of paintings, of photographs, or of sculptures?
3. What do you think will happen if Michael enters the competition and loses?
4. What kind of painting, if any, do you like most?
5. Have you ever entered a competition?
6. Do you feel that competition is good because it encourages excellence, or bad because it discourages the losers, or that it has both positive and negative aspects?

USING YOUR ENGLISH

Confusing similarities between the ACTIVE and the PASSIVE VOICES

A. Unfortunately, the active and passive forms of the present perfect and present continuous tenses look very much alike. Students frequently find these similarities confusing. Study the examples below. You will see how to combine auxiliaries correctly to create many different combinations of tenses and voices.

Examples:

They *have repaired* the road recently.	ACTIVE: Present Perfect
The road *has been repaired* recently.	PASSIVE: Present Perfect
The road *is being repaired* now.	PASSIVE: Present Continuous
The state *is repairing* the road now.	ACTIVE: Present Continuous
They *have been repairing* the road recently.	ACTIVE: Present Perfect Continuous

B. Tell whether the following are ACTIVE or PASSIVE.

1. I've been robbed! _____
2. I've been having a good time. _____
3. John has been doing the job slowly. _____
4. The job is being done slowly. _____
5. Mary has been in Europe on business. _____
6. Mary has been going to Europe on business for years. _____
7. Mary has gone to Europe on business. _____
8. Mary has been sent to Europe on business. _____

As you can see, the general rule is:

HAVE + _____ ed = ACTIVE

BE + _____ ing = ACTIVE

HAVE + BE + _____ ing = ACTIVE

BE + _____ ed = PASSIVE

HAVE + BE _____ ed = PASSIVE

C. In the following exercise, choose the right answer(s) to each question.

1. Which is impossible?
   a. I've been eating a lot recently.
   b. I've been eaten a lot recently.

2. Which two have similar meanings?
   a. I've been robbed.
   b. I've been a robber.
   c. I've been robbing people.

3. In which one is Tom guilty of cheating?
   a. Tom has been cheated.
   b. Tom has been cheating.

4. Which mugging is still happening?
   a. Police! Somebody is being mugged!
   b. Police! Somebody has been mugged!

5. In which sentence does 's mean "has"?
   a. My apartment's been robbed!
   b. My apartment's being robbed!

6. In which sentence is the speaker joking?
   a. I've been fooled.
   b. I've been a fool.
   c. I've been fooling.

7. In which one am I innocent of cheating?
   a. I've been cheating.
   b. I've been cheated.
   c. I've been a cheat.

8. In which one is Mary an artist?
   a. Mary's been painting.
   b. Mary's been painted.
   c. Mary's being painted.

9. Which one is impossible?
   a. The letter's already been written.
   b. The letter's already been writing.

10. In which does 's mean "is"?
   a. Mary's been driven home by John.
   b. Mary's been driving John home.
   c. Mary's being driven home by John.

UNIT 46
The Birthday Party

LESSON 1

811 EVERYONE: *Happy Birthday to you,
Happy Birthday to you,
Happy Birthday, dear Ali,
Happy Birthday to you.

MRS. NIKZAD: Blow out the candles, Ali, but first make a wish.
812 ALI: What should I wish for?
BILL: Anything you want, but don't tell us. If you tell your wish, it won't come true. [*Ali blows out the candles on the cake.*]
HUSSEIN: Here comes the ice cream!
ALI: Wow, look at it all! Gallons and gallons of it!
813 MRS. NIKZAD: [*to Bill*] You know, Mr. O'Neill, by the time we left the house, Ali had asked for ice cream at least half a dozen times.₈₁₃ I'm glad I didn't let him have any.
814 WAITER: [*to Ali*] Here you are. And here's a big spoon.
REPORTER: [*to all*] Hold it. Just like that! [*There is a flash from the camera.*] Now another one, Ali. Hold that spoon up. Good. [*There is another flash.*] Thank you.
815 [*to Mr. Nikzad*] I hadn't expected such a big turnout.₈₁₅ Thanks for the story.
ALI: Who is that, Dad?
816 MR. NIKZAD: A reporter for *The World's Fair Newsletter*.
ALI: Wow! Will my picture be in the papers?
MR. NIKZAD: I hope so.

GRAMMATICAL PREVIEW

The Past Perfect Tense

The past perfect tense signifies that one event occurred before another event in the past. To describe the first event we use the past perfect tense. To describe the second event, we use the simple past tense.

Example: Unfortunately, John *had* already *left* by the time Mary *arrived*.

The phrase *by the time* shows that Mary's arrival is the speaker's point of reference in past time. *Had left* shows that John's departure was farther in the past, before Mary's arrival.

SUBJECTS	PAST PERFECT		SIMPLE PAST
I	**had** already **left**	when Mary	arrived.
You	**eaten**		
We	**gone** to bed		
They	**finished** dinner		
He/She	**started** the meeting		
It	**stopped** raining		

SUBSTITUTION DRILLS

1. Happy Birthday to you,
　　　　　　　to you,
　　　　　　　dear Ali,
　　　　　　　to you.

2. What should I wish for? —Wish for anything you want.
　　　　　　　　　　　　whatever you like.
　　　　　　　　　　　　an easy final exam.
　　　　　　　　　　　　a victory for the team. .

3. He had asked for some ice cream.
 Suzy   hot coffee.
 Peggy and I   fresh bread.
 You   new clothes.
 They   money.

4. You know, by the time we left the house
 Ali had **asked for ice cream**   at least six times.
     called the ice cream parlor
     tried to find his presents
     fought with Hussein
     wanted to call you
     put on and taken off his coat

5. a. I'm glad I didn't let him have any ice cream.
        her
        them
        you

 b. I'm glad I didn't let him **have any.**
         stay by himself.
         come in.
         read the letter.
         get into a fight.

6. I   hadn't expected such a big turnout.
 The reporter
 She
 We
 The Nikzads

7. I hadn't   **expected such a big turnout.**
         counted on so many people coming.
         imagined there would be such a crowd.
         heard of an ice cream party before.
         thought it would be a very good story.

8. Who is that, Dad?
    —**A reporter for The World's Fair Newsletter.**
     An investigator for the insurance company.
     A consultant to the bank.
     An advisor to the President.
     An inspector from the Board of Health.

CONNECTED DRILL

Had   **you expected such a big turnout?**
        you and Zahra reserved the Ice Cream Parlor?
        the Nikzads already arrived when you got there?
        Ali seen any of his gifts before the party?
        Mrs. Nikzad met the reporter before this afternoon?

       — **Yes,** I   **had.**
              we
              they

       — **No,** he   **hadn't.**
              she

EXERCISES

1. Use the simple past tense and the past perfect tense in each of the sentences below. Use the past perfect to describe the action that came first in time.

> **Example:** By the time we (*leave*) the house, Ali (*ask*) for ice cream at least half a dozen times.
>
> *By the time we <u>left</u> the house, Ali <u>had asked</u> for ice cream at least half a dozen times.*

a. Claire (*work*) for two years as a saleswoman before she (*get*) the job with Mr. Crawford.

b. Paulo (*go*) to Chicago last week. He (*be*) there once before on business a few years ago.

c. Nora and Bill (*know*) each other for three years when Bill (*become*) an undercover agent.

d. By the time Hussein (*start*) school, he (*learn*) to write his name and to count to a hundred.

e. We (*watch*) an old love story on television last night, even though we (*see*) it twice before.

2. Change the simple past to the past perfect, using the information in parentheses.

Example: Henry didn't expect such a big turnout. (*before he came to the party*)

Henry hadn't expected such a big turnout before he came to the party.

a. Ali never had his picture in the paper. (*before Henry Leeds interviewed him*)

b. Miguel forgot what life was like back home. (*by the time he was ready to return to Colombia*)

c. Joana didn't think very much about marriage. (*until she met Michael*)

d. Mrs. Nikzad didn't realize how many people knew Ali. (*before she wrote out the guest list*)

e. The waiter didn't finish setting the tables. (*by the time the first guests arrived*)

3. Give affirmative or negative short answers to the questions.

Examples: 1. Did Ali keep his wish a secret? (*yes*)
Yes, he did.

2. Had the Nikzads met Henry Leeds before the day of the party? (*no*)
No, they hadn't.

a. Did all the guests have a good time at the party? (*yes*)

b. Had you and Bill ever tasted banana ice cream before? (*no*)

c. Was Joana at Ali's party? (*no*)

d. Had you had any special training before you took the job? (*yes*)

e. Had Hussein started school before the Nikzads came to the United States? (*yes*)

f. Was the weather hot while I was away on vacation? (*yes*)

g. Had Mrs. Nikzad tried to make Ali take a nap before they went to the Ice Cream Parlor? (*yes*)

h. Had Laura found another job before she quit her old one? (*no*)

i. Did Ali blow out all the candles on his birthday cake? (*yes*)

LESSON 2

817 ALI: I wish I hadn't eaten dinner last night.

MRS. NIKZAD: Why, Ali? Don't you feel well?

ALI: Oh, no! I feel fine. But I wish I had room for more ice cream.

818 MRS. NIKZAD: I hope you don't get sick.

819 ALI: I won't. But even if I do, I won't be sorry. **819**

820 HUSSEIN: I wish I had known about this place for *my* birthday. **820** Ali, open your presents. Here's one from Mr. Yamamoto.

ALI: O.K. [*He tears the wrapping paper off the first present.*] Wow! A baseball and a bat. Gee, thank you, Mr. Yamamoto.

821 HUSSEIN: Here's one from Mr. O'Neill. I wonder if it's a giant ice cream sandwich! **821**

822 ALI: Oh, boy! I wish it were my birthday every day! **822**

823 MR. NIKZAD: I'm glad it's not.

ALI: Wow, a mitt!

HUSSEIN: Here's a note. I'll read it to you.

824

Dear Ali,

You don't know me, but my father says you're an okay kid, and you want to learn to play baseball. O.K., I'll teach you. Happy Birthday.

Bill, Jr.

P.S. I wish I could have come to your party.

825 ALI: Wow! I wish we had invited everybody in the world! **825**

SUBSTITUTION DRILLS

1. I hope **you don't get sick.**
he remembers the way here.
she didn't forget anything.
he has already registered for classes.
you haven't been waiting long.

2. Even if I **do,**   I won't be sorry.
get sick,
get in trouble,
lose my job,
hurt her feelings,

3. I wonder if it's a **giant ice cream sandwich!**
pair of roller skates!
chemistry set!
model airplane!
jigsaw puzzle!

4. I wish **we had invited everybody in the world!**
this day would never end!
I could be a child forever!
you could have seen the look on Ali's face!
you hadn't gone to so much trouble.

CONNECTED DRILLS

1. I wish **I had known about this place,** but **I didn't.**
Pedro had brought his guitar,   he didn't.
Nora had had some free time,   she didn't.
the post office had been open,   it wasn't.
Billy could have come to the party,   he couldn't.

2. I wish **I hadn't eaten dinner last night,**   but **I did.**
I hadn't promised to help Nora on Saturday,   I did.
my grandparents hadn't died before I was born,   they did.
the supermarket hadn't been out of milk,   it was.
I hadn't been feeding the baby when you called,   I was.

3. I wish **it were my birthday every day!** —But it isn't,   Ali.
I were a prince.   you're not,
my father were a millionaire.   he isn't,
I had been there to help you.   you weren't,
it hadn't been raining that week.   it was,

4. I wish I **could come**   to your party, but **I can't.**
were coming   I'm not.
could have come   I couldn't.
had come   I didn't.
hadn't come   I did.
had been able to come   I couldn't.

EXERCISES

1. Read the statements. Then make a statement in which you wish for
the opposite.

> **Examples:** 1. I didn't cash my pay check today.
> *I wish I had cashed my pay check today.*
>
> 2. The drugstore wasn't open.
> *I wish the drugstore had been open.*

    a.   I didn't have my car serviced last week.
    b.   The O'Neills weren't home when I called.
    c.   The fish weren't biting today.
    d.   We didn't get tickets for the ballet.
    e.   My old neighborhood wasn't the same as it used to be.

2. Read the statements. Then make a statement in which you wish for the opposite.

> **Examples:** 1. I told a lie.
> *I wish I hadn't told a lie.*
>
> 2. The door was locked.
> *I wish the door hadn't been locked.*
>
> 3. The other children were teasing Ali.
> *I wish the other children hadn't been teasing Ali.*

a. Ali let the cat out.
b. It was too cold to go swimming.
c. Jack was listening to the radio all night long.
d. Michael drove home in a snowstorm.
e. Peggy had her hair cut short.

3. Use the right form of "hope" or "wish" in the sentences.

a. This is a great party. I _____ we had invited everybody in the world!
b. I'm sorry you had a car accident. I _____ no one got hurt.
c. Pedro sold his camera, and now he _____ he hadn't. His old camera took better pictures than his new one does.
d. Joana _____ Michael will win the art competition. If he does, they will be able to be together in Brazil.
e. Ali _____ he can have another birthday party like this one.
f. Billy _____ he could have come to Ali's birthday party. Unfortunately, he has baseball practice every afternoon.
g. I _____ you have a wonderful time on your vacation. Don't forget to send me a card.
h. I'm having such a good time that I _____ I could stay here forever.
i. I _____ she hasn't bought any more magazines. She already has stacks of them all over her room.

UNIT 47
The Unveiling

LESSON 1

[*Michael is showing his painting to Pedro.*]

	MICHAEL:	Do you like it?
	PEDRO:	It's brilliant!
	MICHAEL:	I hope the judges think so.
	PEDRO:	I hate to tell you, but I heard through a friend of a friend that Leo van der Zee is entering the competition.
	MICHAEL:	I wish you hadn't told me.
	PEDRO:	Oh, come on. Your painting is great.
826	MICHAEL:	Sure, but van der Zee is a fine painter, and he's much better known than I.
827	PEDRO:	*So what?
828	MICHAEL:	I guess you're right. But I wish I knew if I was wasting my time.₈₂₈
829	PEDRO:	If you knew what the future was going to be like, life would be boring.
830	MICHAEL:	I didn't know that you had become a philosopher.
831	PEDRO:	And I had forgotten that you could be such a pain in the neck.
	MICHAEL:	You're right. I'm sorry. I'm driving everyone crazy.
832		**Let's change the subject.₈₃₂ Do you have any more bad news?
	PEDRO:	No. That's all for today.

*Informal for "Does that matter?"
**Let's talk about something else.

GRAMMATICAL PREVIEW

If-Clauses that Describe a Present Condition contrary to fact

If he knew what I know, he'd be unhappy.

Pedro is assuming:
   a. Miguel doesn't know what he knows.
   b. Miguel is happy because he doesn't know what Pedro knows.

Pedro is implying all this by suggesting the opposite.
If Miguel knew what Pedro knows (but he doesn't), *he'd be unhappy.*
   (but he isn't)

Here is another example:
If I had a million dollars, I'd quit my job.
   a. I don't have a million dollars.
   b. I won't quit my job because I don't have a million dollars.

Note: These two sentences mean the same thing:

   He'd be unhappy if he knew what I know.
   If he knew what I know, he'd be unhappy.

SUBSTITUTION DRILLS

1. He's much **better known** than I.
            better educated
            better read
            more experienced
            more organized

2. He's much better known than I. — So what?
What difference does it make?
What does it matter?

3. I wish I knew if I was wasting my time.
Pedro was serious.
Miguel could afford to visit.
Joana would agree with me.
Gary was all right.

4. If you knew what the future was going
to be like, life would be boring.
life wouldn't be any fun.
you would be rich.
you could make a lot of money as a fortuneteller.

5. I didn't know you had become a philosopher.
sage.
wise man.
guru.
prophet.

6. I had forgotten you could be such a pain in the neck.
wise guy.
smart aleck.
know-it-all.

7. Let's change the subject.
talk about something else.
get off this topic.
not continue this discussion.

EXERCISES

1. Use "will" to express a real present–future condition or "would" to express an unreal present condition. Use the contractions " 'll" or " 'd" wherever possible.

> **Examples:** 1. If you're hungry, I _____ heat up some soup.
> *If you're hungry, I'll heat up some soup.*
>
> 2. Laura _____ be happy if she could find an interesting job.
> *Laura would be happy if she could find an interesting job.*

a. If you're cold, I _____ close the window.
b. Michael and Joana _____ go on a picnic if the weather were nice.
c. If I knew English better, I _____ n't be afraid to speak it.
d. We _____ eat out tonight if you're too tired to cook dinner.
e. Miguel _____ stay in New York longer if he didn't have to go back to school in Bogotá.
f. If Ali doesn't behave himself, his father _____ send him to his room.

2. Use the correct form of the verb to express an unreal present-future condition.

> **Example:** Joana would enter the competition if she _____ related to Paulo. (*not be*)
> *Joana would enter the competition if she weren't related to Paulo.*

a. If you _____ Mr. Nikzad, what would you get Zahra for her birthday? (*be*)
b. I'd go swimming with you if I _____ a cold. (*not have*)

c. If Claire _____ so busy with school and work, she'd have more time to read for pleasure. (not be)

d. I'd take a trip around the world if I _____ the lottery. (win)

e. What would you do if the airlines _____ your luggage? (lose)

f. If Nora _____ breakfast for her children, she could sleep later. (not have to make)

g. If Paulo _____ how to play bridge, the four of us could have a game after dinner. (know)

h. You wouldn't be able to do this exercise if you _____ English. (not understand)

3. Change the sentences. Use the unreal conditional form.

Example: You'll be upset if I tell you the truth.
You'd be upset if I told you the truth.

a. Henry will lend you some money if you ask him.

b. Joana will be disappointed if you don't come for dinner.

c. I'll leave for Chicago at noon on Friday if I can take the afternoon off.

d. I'll have dessert if I have room for it.

e. Michael will continue painting if he wins the competition.

f. They'll help you if they aren't busy.

g. Mr. and Mrs. Nikzad will go to the movies if they can get a babysitter.

h. I'll go home early if I get tired.

i. We'll have flowers next spring if we plant the bulbs now.

j. You won't have to do your work over again if you do it carefully the first time.

LESSON 2

	PEDRO:	Miguel called Marta from Colombia. He loves her. He misses her. He thinks about her every minute, and he can't live without her. He says.
	MICHAEL:	He's a nice guy.
833	PEDRO:	He's young and inexperienced. If he knew what I know . . . ₈₃₃
834	MICHAEL:	He'd be cynical, old, and unhappy, like you.₈₃₄
835		Leave him alone. If you could find a girl like Marta, you'd be a lucky man.₈₃₅
	PEDRO:	That may be. In any case, he wishes you the best of luck in the competition.
836	MICHAEL:	Thank him for me if you get a chance. By the way, why are you so dressed up today?₈₃₆ It couldn't be just for the unveiling of my painting.₈₃₇
837		
	PEDRO:	Very funny. Actually, I had an interview at a photographic supply house.
	MICHAEL:	I'm impressed.
	PEDRO:	They want me to be the assistant manager of their camera department.
838	MICHAEL:	You? In a nine to five job!₈₃₈ I can't believe it. Pedro in a jacket and tie! I never thought I'd live to see the day.₈₃₉
839		
840	PEDRO:	*Hey, give me a break!
	MICHAEL:	Pedro, I think it's great. Congratulations.
	PEDRO:	Thanks. I guess.
	MICHAEL:	You don't seem very happy about it.
	PEDRO:	I have to get used to the idea.

*Informal for "Stop teasing me."

SUBSTITUTION DRILLS

1. If he knew what I know, he **wouldn't be so idealistic.**
wouldn't rush into marriage.
would be cynical, too.
would appreciate life more.

2. If you could find a girl like Marta, **you'd be a lucky man.**
you'd be a happy man.
you'd get married and live
happily ever after.
you wouldn't stay single very
long.

3. If **you could find a girl like Marta,** you'd be a lucky man.
you won the lottery,
you were never sick,·
everything went smoothly,

4. In any case, he wishes **you the best of luck in the competition.**
you all the best.
Michael success in his career.
them a happy anniversary.
us a safe trip.

5. By the way, why are you **so dressed up**   today?
wearing a suit and tie
in your best clothes
in your Sunday best

6. You? In a **nine to five** job!
full-time
regular

7. Hey, *****give me a break!**
*cut it out!
*knock it off!
stop it!

* informal

8. I never thought I'd live to see the day.
him get married.
him grow up.
them get a divorce.
you get a job.

CONNECTED DRILL

If he knew   what I know . . .
earned   earn . . .
felt   feel . . .
had   have . . .
needed   need . . .
understood   understand . . .

EXERCISES

1. Join the two statements to make one expressing the unreal present-future condition.

Examples: 1. Joana doesn't make fun of Michael. He'd be angry if she did.
Michael'd be angry if Joana made fun of him.

2. I don't tease you about your work. You wouldn't like it if I did.
You wouldn't like it if I teased you about your work.

a. I don't know her address. I'd write to her if I did.
b. Joana doesn't have a nine to five job. She couldn't sleep late if she did.
c. We aren't in a hurry. We'd leave now if we were.
d. I'm not you. I wouldn't do that if I were.
e. Laura doesn't have the patience. She'd be a teacher if she did.
f. She can't get her visa extended. She wouldn't go back home if she could.

g. I don't call Yolanda after midnight. She wouldn't like it if I did.
h. Peggy can't remember John's last name. She'd be able to find his phone number if she could.

2. Make questions and give answers using the information in parentheses as in the examples:

Examples: 1. (have a toothache—go to the dentist)
Question: *What would you do if you had a toothache?*
Answer: *I'd go to the dentist.*

2. (not know anyone in this room—introduce myself)
Question: *What would you do if you didn't know anyone in this room?*
Answer: *I'd introduce myself.*

a. (get lost in a strange city—ask a policeman for directions)
b. (not·understand this exercise—study the lesson again)
c. (the bus drivers go on strike—stay home from work)
d. (the phone doesn't work—report it to the telephone company)
e. (not know the spelling of a word—look it up in the dictionary)
f. (have three wishes—wish for health, wealth, and three more wishes)

3. Use "wish" instead of "hope" in the sentences below. Make whatever other changes are required. Follow the example.

Example: I hope that he has the best of luck in the competition.
I wish him the best of luck in the competition.

a. **We hope he has** a successful career.
b. **She hopes they have** a safe trip.
c. **I hope you have** a happy retirement.
d. **He hopes she has** a long and healthy life.
e. **They hope we have** a happy new year.

UNIT 48
Still Looking

LESSON 1

LAURA: Hello, Bill.

BILL: How are you, Laura? Have you found a job yet?

CUSTOMER: Do you have vanilla cones?

BILL: Certainly. Here you are.

841   [*to Laura*] Now, where were we? Oh, yes. I asked if you had found a job yet.₈₄₁

LAURA: No, not yet, but I've been doing a lot of thinking.

BILL: Well, you know Paulo Farias, the nice-looking young man at the Brazilian Pavilion?

LAURA: Yes, I remember him.

842 BILL: I told him that you had resigned.

LAURA: You did?

843 BILL: And that you were looking for a new position.

LAURA: What did he say?

844 BILL: He said that he remembered you.

845 LAURA: That's nice. What else did he say?₈₄₅

846 BILL: He said he was looking for a secretary. But he also

847   said he didn't think he could hire you.

LAURA: Oh, why?

848 BILL: Because he does a lot of work with Mr. Crawford's office.

LAURA: Yes, of course. Oh, well, thanks for trying.

GRAMMATICAL PREVIEW

Reported Speech

When reporting or saying what another person has already said, it is usually necessary to change the verb tense and the subject pronoun of the original sentence.

> **Example:**   Laura said, "I'm looking for a job."
> What did she say?
> *She said she was looking for a job.*
> *She told Bill she was looking for a job.*

The verb tense is changed to a time farther in the past, from *am looking* to *was looking*, and the subject pronoun also must be changed from *I* to *she*.

ORIGINAL	*REPORTED SPEECH*
1. *Present*	
He said, "I **want** to go to the opera."	He said he **wanted** to go to the opera.
He said, "I'**m** angry."	He said he **was** angry.
2. *With modals*	
He said, "I **can** meet you tomorrow."	He said he **could** meet me tomorrow.
He said, "I'**ll** give you a ride."	He said he *****would** give me a ride.
He said, "I **may** work late."	He said he **might** work late.
He said, "I **must** finish some work."	He said he **had to** finish some work.
3. *Past*	
He said, "I **went** to work yesterday."	He said he **had gone** to work yesterday.
He said, "I **was** in Rome in 1976."	He said he **had been** in Rome in 1976.

Note that *would* is the past tense of *will*.

4. *Present Perfect*
   He said, "I**'ve been** to Paris."   He said he **had been** to Paris.

5. *Yes/No Questions* and *Wh-Questions* make the same changes in
   verb tenses and pronouns, but you change the question order to
   a statement word order.
   He asked me, "**Are** you   He asked me if I **was** happy.
   happy?"

Exceptions:
We do not change the tense of the verb:

   a.   When reporting the imperative.
   b.   When reporting the past perfect. (It cannot go back farther in
        the past.)
   c.   When reporting scientific facts (and some other kinds of facts -
        see Refocus Unit 50).

*SUBSTITUTION DRILLS

1. I asked you, *"Have you found*   a job yet?"
         if you had found   a job yet.
         , "Have you written   your résumé yet?"
         if you had written   your résumé yet.
         , "Have you looked   in the want ads?"
         if you had looked   in the want ads.
         , "Have you applied   for a job at the Fair?"
         if you had applied   for a job at the Fair.

2. Bill asked Laura, *"Do you remember*   Paulo Farias?"
         if she remembered   Paulo Farias.
         , "Are you still looking   for a job?"
         if she was still looking   for a job.
         , "Did you go   to the employment agency?"
         if she had gone   to the employment agency.
         , "Have you checked   the want ads?"
         if she had checked   the want ads.

3. *[Bill is speaking to Laura.]*

   I **said,**   **"Laura resigned."**
   told Paulo that *you had resigned.*
   said,   "Laura and I had   a long talk."
   told Paulo that *you and I had had* a long talk.
   said,   "Business was   slow last month."
   told Paulo that *business had been* slow last month.
   said,   "Laura didn't like   the job at Crawford's
                                      agency."
   told Paulo that *you hadn't liked* the job at Crawford's agency.

---

*Many of these substitution drills are different from the others in these books. They are written in pairs and should be drilled in pairs.

4. *[Bill is speaking to Laura.]*

I said,	*"Laura is looking*	**for a new position."**
told Paulo that	*you were looking*	for a new position.
said,	*"You're working*	too hard."
told Paulo that	*he was working*	too hard.
said,	*"I'm*	busy, as usual."
told Paulo that	*I was*	busy, as usual.
said,	*"Jobs are*	hard to find."
told Paulo that	*jobs were*	hard to find.

5. *[Paulo is speaking to Bill.]*

Paulo said,	*"I remember*	Laura."
	that he remembered	you.
	, "My sister helps	me out at the office."
	that his sister helped	him out at the office.
	, "Crawford works	with us on a regular basis."
	that Crawford worked	with them on a regular basis.
	, "I'll give	Laura a hand, if possible."
	that he'd give	you a hand, if possible.

6. What else did **he say?**
- he ask you?
- he want to know?
- you tell him?
- you discuss?

7. *[Paulo is speaking to Bill.]*

Paulo said,	*"I'm looking*	**for a new secretary."**
	that he was looking	for a new secretary.
	, "We're going to open	some new exhibitions."
	that they were going to open	some new exhibitions.
	, "Things are getting	quite busy in the office."
	that things were getting	quite busy in the office.

8. *[Bill is speaking to Laura.]*

Paulo said, *"I don't think I can*   hire Laura."
          that he didn't think he could   hire you.
          , "I can't promise Laura will get   a job."
          that he couldn't promise you would get a job.
          , "I'm not saying Laura can't apply   to another
                                                                   department."
          that he wasn't saying you couldn't apply to another
                                                                   department.

9. *[Paulo is speaking to Bill.]*

Paulo said *, "I do*   **a lot of work with Crawford's
                                                 agency."**
          that he did   a lot of work with Crawford's
                                             agency.
          , "I need   someone right away."
          that he needed someone right away.
          , "I want   to hire someone right away."
          that he wanted to hire someone right away.
          , "I have   to work overtime almost every day."
          that he had   to work overtime almost every day.

EXERCISES

1. Change the direct statements to indirect statements as in the
     examples. For other examples, see the substitution drills.

Examples: 1. LAURA: I remember Paulo.
                       Laura said that she remembered Paulo.

               2. PAULO: My secretary hasn't been feeling well.
                       *Paulo said that his secretary hadn't been feeling
                       well.*

   a. LAURA: I need a job.
   b. BILL: My wife doesn't work on Mondays.

c.   NORA: We're out of roses.

d.   PAULO: I'm not a good dancer.

e.   LAURA: I'm thinking of leaving New York.

f.   JACK: Billy and Peggy aren't helping me.

g.   BILLY: I'm going to give Suzy a record for Christmas.

h.   NORA: The store isn't going to be open on New Year's Day.

i.   MARTA: I got a letter from Miguel.

j.   BILL: Mr. Crawford didn't fire Laura.

k.   JIMMY: Ali's party was a lot of fun.

l.   MIGUEL: Marta cried all the way to the airport.

m   ALI: I was teasing Hussein.

n.   PEDRO: I've decided to take a nine to five job.

o.   MRS. NIKZAD: My husband and I haven't met Ali's teacher.

p.   LAURA: I've been reading the want ads.

q.   MICHAEL: I haven't been sleeping well.

r.   CLAIRE: I can type seventy words a minute.

s.   JOANA: Paulo can't play bridge.

t.   BILL: I'll pick up some groceries on my way home from work.

u.   MRS. CRAWFORD: The car won't start.

v.   MR. NIKZAD: Ali must eat his lunch.

2. Change the direct questions to reported speech. In this exercise, Laura is telling Bill about her first visit to an employment agency.

Example: INTERVIEWER [*to Laura*]: Do you have any secretarial experience?
She asked me if I had any secretarial experience.

a.   "Did you see our ad in the Sunday paper?"
b.   "Did someone refer you to us?"
c.   "Have you filled out an application?"
d.   "Have you registered with any other employment agencies?"
e.   "Do you have a résumé?"
f.   "Are you a college graduate?"
g.   "Are you in good health?"
h.   "Can you type?"
i.   "Can you take shorthand?"
j.   "Were you your last employer's personal secretary?"
k.   "Will you be able to start work right away?"
l.   "Will you accept a job in another city?"
m.   "Are you willing to relocate?"
n.   "Do you know how to drive?"
o.   "Do you own a car?"
p.   "Is there a number where you can be reached?"

LESSON 2

849 BILL: Wait, don't give up yet. He said he might be able to find you a job in another department.₈₄₉

LAURA: Oh, Bill. You're wonderful. Thank you. You should open up an employment agency.

850 BILL: That's what my wife says. That reminds me, she asked me to pick up a few things on the way home.₈₅₀

LAURA: Does your wife work, too?

BILL: Yes, she's a florist.

LAURA: Does she like it?

851 BILL: Yes, she was saying just last night that she had never enjoyed a job more.₈₅₁ So now, what are we going

852   to do about you? You said that you had been doing a lot of thinking.₈₅₂

853 LAURA: Yes, I was thinking that maybe I needed a change.

854 BILL: Have you ever thought about being a tour guide?

LAURA: A tour guide?

855 BILL: Someone told me that he had heard that they needed another Spanish-English tour guide.₈₅₅ Even though they haven't announced the opening yet, I'd apply now.

LAURA: Maybe I should. You really are a sweetheart.

BILL: Good luck.

SUBSTITUTION DRILLS

1. *[Bill is talking to Laura in the second sentence of each pair.]*

Paulo	said,	*"I may be*	able to find Laura a job."
	told me	*he might be*	able to find you a job.
	said,	*"There may be*	an opening soon."
	told me	*there might be*	an opening soon.
	said,	*"I'll know*	more about it in a few weeks."
	told me	*he would know*	more about it in a few weeks.
	said,	*"You should open*	up an employment agency."
	told me	*I should open*	up an employment agency.

2. Nora

	said,	*"Pick up*	a few things on the way home."
	asked me	*to pick up*	a few things on the way home.
	said,	*"Don't be*	late for dinner."
	asked me	*not to be*	late for dinner.
	said,	*"Stop by*	the flower shop around 5 o'clock."
	asked me	*to stop by*	the flower shop around 5 o'clock.
	said,	*"Don't forget*	to pay the telephone bill."
	asked me	*not to forget*	to pay the telephone bill.
	said,	*"Don't make*	any plans for the weekend."
	told me	*not to make*	any plans for the weekend.

3. Laura asked Bill

, **"Does your wife work, too?"**
if his wife worked, too.
, "Where does she work?"
where she worked.
, "How does she like the job?"
how she liked the job.
, "Who does she work for?"
who she worked for.
, "Why does she want to work?"
why she wanted to work.

4. Nora was saying just last night
that she had never enjoyed a job more.
had such a great job.
met so many people.
handled so much responsibility.
felt so self-confident.
enjoyed a job so much.

5. Laura said,   *"I've been doing* a lot of thinking."
Bill reminded her,   *"You said you had been doing* a lot of thinking."
Laura said,   *"I've been thinking* about going back to school."
Bill reminded her,   *"You said you had been thinking* about going back to school."
Laura said,   *"I haven't been feeling* well lately."
Bill reminded her,   *"You said you hadn't been feeling* well lately."
Laura said,   *"I haven't been sleeping* much recently."
Bill reminded her,   *"You said you hadn't been sleeping* much recently."

6. I was thinking that maybe I needed a change.
I ought to leave New York.
I shouldn't have resigned.
you could help me find a job.
I should take a vacation.

7. Have you ever thought of being a tour guide?
a translator?
an interpreter?
a counselor?
a consultant?

8. Someone told me that
he had heard that they needed another tour guide.
his boss had said
a friend of his had mentioned
he had read

EXERCISES

1. Change the direct commands to reported speech as in the examples.

> **Examples:** 1. Nora said to Bill, Jr., "Buy a loaf of bread and a quart of milk on your way home from school."
> *Nora told Bill, Jr. to buy a loaf of bread and a quart of milk on his way home from school.*
>
> 2. Nora said to Peggy, "Don't be late for dinner."
> *Nora told Peggy not to be late for dinner.*
>
> 3. Bill said to Laura, "Would you watch my cart for a minute?"
> *Bill asked Laura to watch his cart for a minute.*

a. Bill said to Peggy, "Turn down the television."
b. Michael said to Pedro, "Don't be so cynical."
c. Paulo said to Joana, "Would you pass the salt and pepper?"
d. Hussein said to Ali, "Don't bother me."
e. Nora said to Jack, "Straighten up your room."
f. The interviewer said to Laura, "Would you fill out an application?"
g. Mrs. Farias said to Joana, "Would you hold the door for me?"
h. Billy said to Jack, "Save me a seat on the bus."
i. Pedro said to Miguel, "Don't forget to write."

2. Change the direct questions to reported speech as in the example.

> **Example:** Michael asked, "Where do you live?"
> *Michael asked me where I lived.*

a. The professor asked, "What courses are you taking?"
b. Michael asked Joana, "When can I see you again?"
c. My mother asked, "Who did you go to the movies with?"
d. The American asked, "How long have you been studying English?"

e. My friend asked, "Where are you going to get your hair cut?"
f.• Ali asked, "When is your birthday?"
g. My neighbor asked, "Who were you just talking to?"
h. My boss asked, "When do you plan to take your vacation?"
i. The hotel clerk asked, "How long will you be in New York?"
j. The parking lot attendant asked, "What kind of car do you have?"

3. Change the direct statements or questions to reported speech. Remember to change the time or place expressions, too.

Examples: 1. Michael said, "I didn't get much sleep **last night**." (*the night before*)
Michael said he hadn't gotten much sleep the night before.

2. Mrs. Ortega called Miguel in New York and asked, "Will you be **here** on Tuesday or Wednesday?" (*there*)
Mrs. Ortega called Miguel in New York and asked him if he would be there on Tuesday or Wednesday.

a. When Mrs. Ortega phoned Miguel from Colombia, she said, "It's been raining **here** for a week." (*there*)
b. A couple of days ago, Peggy remembered her parents' anniversary. She wasn't sure of the date so she asked her mother, "Is **tomorrow** your anniversary?" (*the next day*)
c. When Michael told Joana about Gary, he said, "Gary left home **several years ago**." (*several years before*)
d. I saw Pedro two weeks ago. He wanted me to call him, but he said, "Don't call me after ten o'clock **this evening**." (*that evening*)
e. When I saw Pedro, he was very busy. But he said, "I won't be busy **next week**." (*the following week*)
f. I wondered why Pedro was so busy, so I asked him, "What have you been doing **this week**?" (*that*)
g. Last night I saw Marta at the movies. She said, "I ran into Marian in the supermarket **this morning**." (*that morning*)

h. The day before yesterday, Joana told Paulo, "Meet me in front of the post office after work **today**." (*that day*)

i. Last Tuesday Michael had an appointment with Paulo, but he forgot about it. On Wednesday, Paulo asked Joana, "Where was Michael **yesterday**?" (*the day before*)

4. Here is a conversation between Miguel and Marta. Miguel has been back in Bogotá for three weeks and he is calling Marta long distance.

[*The phone rings.*]

MARTA: Hello?

MIGUEL: Hi, Marta.

MARTA: Miguel! Where are you? How are you? Are you all right?

MIGUEL: Slow down! I'm home and I'm fine. I miss you.

MARTA: I miss you, too. How are things at home?

MIGUEL: All right, I guess. Maybe I'm just depressed because you're not here. But I'd certainly rather be there than here.

MARTA:	Have you started school yet?
MIGUEL:	No, not yet. I registered this morning, but classes don't begin until next week.
MARTA:	Maybe you'll feel better when your mind is occupied.
MIGUEL:	And how are you?
MARTA:	Oh, just about the same. A little depressed. But I pretend that you are still here and with luck, I'll meet you on the stairs.
OPERATOR:	Your three minutes are up, sir.
MIGUEL:	Thank you, operator. [*to Marta*] I have to go. Good-bye, I love you.
MARTA:	Good-bye, Miguel. I love you, too. Take care of yourself.
MIGUEL:	Good-bye. [*He hangs up.*]

Now retell the conversation by filling in this passage.

Marta asked Miguel _____ , _____ , and if _____ all right. He told her _____ . He said that _____ at home, that _____ fine and that _____ . Marta said that _____ , too and then asked Miguel _____ at home. He guessed that _____ all right, but added that maybe _____ because _____ . He told her that _____ certainly rather _____ . Marta wanted to know if _____ school yet. Miguel said that _____ . He said that _____ morning, but that _____ until _____ week. Marta told him that maybe _____ better when _____ .

Then Miguel asked Marta _____ . She replied that _____ just about the same and added that _____ . Then she told Miguel what she did to try to cheer herself up. She said that _____ , and that with luck, _____ on the stairs.

The operator interrupted Miguel's and Marta's conversation to tell Miguel that _____ . Miguel thanked the operator and told Marta that _____ . Then he said good-bye and whispered that _____ . Marta said good-bye and told him that _____ , too. She ended their conversation by reminding Miguel _____ .

UNIT 49
The Judgment

LESSON 1

JOANA: There's quite a crowd here.

MICHAEL: Everybody in the art world is here. Artists, critics, collectors, everybody. I want to go home. There's Leo van der Zee!

PEDRO: Which painting is his?

MICHAEL: The large one to the left of mine. It's very good. Very good.

JOANA: I don't like it.

856   MICHAEL: I would be proud to say that I had done it.

PEDRO: I don't like it, either.

MICHAEL: Ssh. There's Paulo. Did anyone tell him that I
            entered the competition under another name?

857   JOANA: I don't know. But even if he had found out, he
            certainly wouldn't have told me.₈₅₇ Paulo can be
            very discreet.

[*We hear Paulo speaking in the background.*]

858   PAULO: Ladies and gentlemen . . .

[*The people in the room slowly stop talking.*]

859   MICHAEL: Why doesn't he get on with it?

JOANA: Be patient, Michael.

PAULO: . . . The Brazilian Pavilion has been pleased and
            honored to have as judges persons of such
            distinction that . . .

860   MICHAEL: If I had known there were going to be a lot of
            speeches, I would have come later.

JOANA: It'll all be over soon, Michael.

861   PAULO: The judges, as you can imagine, had a very difficult
            time choosing a winner.₈₆₁ The quality of the
            paintings . . .

MICHAEL: [*to himself*] Paulo, shut up. Or say something

862   original. Say something like, "Most of the paintings
            were garbage."₈₆₂

863   PAULO: And if I had been one of the judges, I don't think I
            could have come to any decision at all; but,
            fortunately . . .

864   MICHAEL: I've got to step outside. I need some fresh air.₈₆₄

JOANA: Don't leave now, Michael, they're . . .

MICHAEL: I've got to. I'm too nervous. [*Michael leaves the
            room.*]

GRAMMATICAL PREVIEW

If-Clauses that Describe a Past Condition
contrary to fact

*If I had known there were going to be a lot of speeches,
I would have come later.*

The facts are:
    a.   Michael did not know there were going to be a lot of speeches.

    b.   He came early and heard more speeches than he wanted to.

*If Michael had known there were going to be a lot of speeches, he
would have come later.* (but he didn't know, so he came on time)

Here are some common patterns to illustrate the structure.

    a.   If I *had seen* you, I *would've said* hello. (but I didn't see you,
        so I didn't say hello)
    b.   If I *had known* the answer, I *wouldn't have asked* the
        question. (but I didn't know it, so I asked)
    c.   If I *had invested* in that company years ago, I *would be* rich
        now. (but I didn't invest in it, so I'm not rich)

Note: These two sentences mean the same thing:

        *I would have come later if I had known there were
        going to be so many speeches.*
        *If I had known there were going to be so many
        speeches, I would have come later.*

SUBSTITUTION DRILLS

1. But, if Paulo had **found out,**
            known that Michael was using a pseudonym,
            learned who the real "Pedro Ortega" was,
            discovered "Pedro Ortega's" identity,

  he certainly wouldn't have told Joana.

2. But even if Paulo had found out, he **wouldn't have told me.**
                        wouldn't have breathed a
                        word of it.
                        would have kept it a secret.
                        wouldn't have mentioned it to
                        anyone else.

3. **Ladies and gentlemen** . . .
  Friends and neighbors . . .
  Boys and girls . . .
  Honored guests and distinguished colleagues . . .

4. Why doesn't he **get on with it?**
          dispense with the formalities?
          get to the point?
          forget the small talk?

5. If I had known there were going to be a lot of speeches,

I	would have	come later. arrived an hour later. stayed at the restaurant longer.
	wouldn't have	hurried to get there on time. rushed through dinner.

6. If I

had	known there were going to be a lot of speeches, thought the speeches would go on for an hour,
hadn't	wanted to hear Paulo's speech, been in charge of the competition,

   I would have come late.

7. The judges, **as you can imagine,** had a very difficult time
                                        choosing a winner.
          as you all know,
          it goes without saying,
          needless to say,
          as you would expect,

8. Say something original **like,**   "Most of the paintings were
                                        garbage."
                          such as,
                          to the effect that,

9. If I **had been one of the judges,**
          had had to choose,
          had been asked to select the winner,
          hadn't consulted with the other judges,

   I don't think I could have come to any decision at all.

10. If I had been one of the judges,

I don't think I could have come to any decision at all.

could have chosen between Mr. Van der Zee
and Mr. Ortega.

could have made up my mind.

would have known which painting to select.

11. I need some fresh air.

a change of scenery.

a cigarette.

a shoulder to cry on.

CONNECTED DRILL

I would be	proud	to say that I had	done it.
	pleased		recommended him for the job.
	honored		been a part of the project.
	embarrassed		spent so much time on the report.
	reluctant		worked for Mr. Crawford.

EXERCISES

1. Finish the sentences by selecting the correct second part.

Examples: 1. Even if Paulo had found out,
            a. he wouldn't tell his sister.
            b. he wouldn't have told his sister.
            Even if Paulo had found out, he wouldn't have told his sister.

        2. I would drive you home
            a. if you needed a ride.
            b. if you had needed a ride.
            I would drive you home if you needed a ride.

a. Laura wouldn't have gotten a headache
        1. if she had worn her glasses.
        2. if she wore her glasses.
b. If Miguel had his way,
        1. he would stay in New York.
        2. he would have stayed in New York.
c. They could borrow money from us
        1. if they had wanted to.
        2. if they wanted to.

d. If I had gone to the dentist's sooner,
    1. he could save my tooth.
    2. he could have saved my tooth.
e. Mrs. Nikzad might not have invited Mr. Yamamoto to Ali's party
    1. if Ali hadn't insisted on it.
    2. if Ali didn't insist on it.

2. Use the correct form of the verb to express the past unreal conditional.

Examples: 1. (*be able to*) If Miguel _____ stay in New York, he would have.
    If Miguel had been able to stay in New York, he would have.

    2. (*not be able to*) Joana would have been upset if she _____ attend the ceremonies.
    Joana would have been upset if she hadn't been able to attend the ceremonies.

a. (*know*) If I _____ that everybody in the art world was going to be here, I would have been even more nervous.
b. (*not resign*) Mr. Crawford would probably have fired Laura if she _____.

c. (*be able to*) If Paulo _____ hire Laura, he would have.

d. (*not see*) I would have thought the witness was lying if I _____ the accident myself.

e. (*be*) Michael and his father could have had a closer relationship if Mr. Crawford _____ a different kind of person.

f. (*not tell*) If you _____ me that you were a grandmother, I would never have guessed it.

g. (*not work*) Michael might not have finished his painting by the deadline if he _____ day and night.

h. (*offer*) If he _____ me a job, I would have taken it.

3. Change the sentences to express the past unreal conditional.

> **Examples:** 1. If I were one of the judges, I wouldn't know which
> painting to select.
> *If I had been one of the judges, I wouldn't have
> known which painting to select.*
>
> 2. Michael would go home if Pedro and Joana didn't
> stop him.
> *Michael would have gone home if Pedro and Joana
> hadn't stopped him.*

a. If Michael's father weren't against Michael's career, he would
   enter the competition under his own name.
b. If it weren't for Joana, Michael might not want to win so badly.
c. Pedro could take a picture of Michael's painting if he brought
   his camera.
d. If I didn't really like his painting, I would tell him.
e. You wouldn't recognize Gary if you saw him.
f. They could hold the ceremony outside if it were summer.
g. If you asked me what to do, I wouldn't know what to tell you.

LESSON 2

[Outside in the hall]

	ALI:	Hello. Are you an artist?
865	MICHAEL:	I don't know. The judges are making up their minds. ₈₆₅ Watch it, your ice cream is dripping.
	ALI:	Thanks. Speeches are really boring, aren't they?
866	MICHAEL:	You can say that again. ₈₆₆ That ice cream looks good. Where did you get it?
867	ALI:	Here. Have a bite. ₈₆₇
	MICHAEL:	Uh . . .
	ALI:	Go ahead. I don't mind.
	JOANA:	Michael, quick! They're about to announce the winner.
	MICHAEL:	Excuse me. Thanks for the offer.
	ALI:	Sure.
	PAULO:	. . . And now it is my pleasure to announce the winner. For personal reasons, the artist chose to enter the competition under another name . . .
	JOANA:	It's you! You won! I can't believe . . .

MICHAEL: It could be someone else, too.

868 PAULO: . . . But whatever his name, there can be no
869   doubt that he is a master. The world can
                  expect great things from his brush . . .

MICHAEL: Enough. Enough.

PAULO: The winner, Pedro Ortega. I hope he is here.
              [*The room fills with applause. Michael walks to
              the front of the room and stands next to
              Paulo.*]

870 JOANA: [*to Pedro*] I'm so happy. I don't know what I
                  would have done if Paulo had said some other
                  name. **870**

ALI: I was talking to that man.

MRS. NIKZAD: He's a great painter.

ALI: He likes ice cream, too.

SUBSTITUTION DRILLS

1. The judges are making up their minds.
          deciding.
          coming to a decision.
          reaching a decision.

2. Speeches are really boring, aren't they? —You can say that again.
It's stuffy in here, isn't it?
The hall is packed, isn't it?
Speeches are really dull, aren't they?
Paulo is nervous, isn't he?

3. Have a bite.
      taste.
      lick.
      sip.
      piece.

4. But whatever his name, there can be no doubt that he is a master.
          there can be no question
          it is clear
          it is apparent

5. But whatever his name, there can be no doubt that he is a master.
whoever he is,
wherever he comes from,
whatever name he uses,

6. The world can expect great things from his brush.
          chisel.
          pen.
          baton.
          drawing board.

7. I don't know what
I would have done if **Paulo had said some other name.**
the judges hadn't chosen Michael.
Paulo hadn't said your name.
Leo van der Zee had won.
Michael had lost.

8. Would **Michael and Joana have found a way to stay together**
Michael have gone into business with his father
Michael's father have said, "I told you so,"
this story have had a happy ending

if his painting hadn't been chosen?

9. How would you have felt if **Leo van der Zee had won?**
Michael's painting hadn't been chosen?
Ali hadn't been eating ice cream?

EXERCISES

1. Restate the sentences in the past unreal conditional using "if" and "not."

> **Examples:** 1. I got wet because I forgot my umbrella.
> *If I hadn't forgotten my umbrella, I wouldn't have gotten wet.*
>
> 2. Michael probably didn't take a bite of Ali's ice cream because he didn't know Ali.
> *If he had known Ali, Michael probably would have taken a bite of Ali's ice cream.*

a. The taxi ran into the other car because the driver of that car went through a red light.

b. I wasn't able to start a fire because the wood that I tried to use was wet.

c. Peggy's plants grew fast because she put them in a sunny window.

d. Ali didn't like the speeches because they were boring.

e. Claire didn't do the ironing because she got home late.

f. He took a second job because he needed the money.

2. For each situation below, make a question with "What would have happened if . . . ?" and answer it.

Examples: 1. Michael went out for some fresh air, so he met Ali.
Q. *What would have happened if Michael hadn't gone out for some fresh air?*
A. *If Michael hadn't gone out for some fresh air, he wouldn't have met Ali.*

2. Gary wasn't at the ceremony, so he couldn't congratulate Michael.
Q. *What would have happened if Gary had been at the ceremony?*
A. *If Gary had been at the ceremony, he could have congratulated Michael.*

a. I didn't have the time, so I didn't paint the apartment myself.
b. Joana went out to get Michael so he wouldn't miss hearing the judges' decision.
c. Michael didn't lose the competition, so he didn't have to go into business with his father.
d. I didn't wear a warm coat to the football game, so I was cold all afternoon.
e. Peggy watered her plants so they wouldn't die.
f. Marta was in a hurry, so she forgot to lock the door.
g. We didn't take the map with us, so we got lost.
h. Michael was at the ceremony, so Pedro didn't accept the award for him.

UNIT 50
Reading and Refocus

LESSON 1

THE WORLD'S FAIR NEWSLETTER
Volume 2 No. 1

Published by THE WORLD'S FAIR CORP.
and the G. W. CRAWFORD AGENCY, INC.

A BIRTHDAY AT THE FAIR   by Henry Leeds

871   Today was an important day at the Fair. A guy is seven
872   only once and Ali Nikzad made the most of it.₈₇₁ What is
     closer to a boy's heart than ice cream and baseball?₈₇₂
873   Nothing. And so, at Ali's birthday party there was plenty of
     ice cream and lots of baseball equipment.₈₇₃

874   Ali, the son of Mr. Simon Nikzad, a vice-president of the International Bank, has always loved the Fair and spends all his free time here. **874** He is an independent guy and insists on exploring the world by himself.

875   Ali told this reporter that he'd been dreaming of his
876   birthday for weeks. **875** Had his birthday been everything he
877   could have hoped for? **876** Absolutely. Had he been given everything his heart desired? **877** Definitely.
        And what about friends? They were all there.

878   One of Ali's best friends, Mr. Bill O'Neill, an ice cream
879   vendor here at the Fair, was at the big party. **878** So was Mr. Kenji Yamamoto, whose well-known vegetable market is near the Fair. **879** Naturally Mr. and Mrs. Nikzad were there, and so was Hussein, Ali's older brother. Some of Ali's classmates
880   were there, too, but no girls. When I asked Ali about this, he said, "I don't know anything about girls yet, but I am going to learn about them this year." **880**

Questions about "A Birthday at the Fair"

Fact:
The answers are *clear* in the story.
1. Does Henry Leeds think there is anything closer to a seven-year-old boy's heart than baseball and ice cream?
2. What does Ali do with all his free time?
3. Does Ali prefer to go on adventures by himself or to play with other children?
4. How long had Ali been dreaming of his seventh birthday?
5. Were all of the guests approximately Ali's age except for his parents?
6. Is Ali interested in girls now, or does he plan on finding out about them soon?

Inference:
You can *guess the right answers* from the story.
1. Why weren't there any girls at Ali's birthday party?
2. Does the International Bank have more than one vice-president or only one?
3. Does the reporter approve of Ali's "independence"?
4. Would Ali have changed anything about his party if he had planned it himself?
5. Could Ali have enjoyed his party more?
6. How does the reporter talk to Ali, as if he were an adult or a child?

To the Student:
There are *no wrong answers* to these questions.
1. Why do you think Mr. Leeds reports a child's birthday as if it were an important event?
2. Are seven-year-old boys in your country interested in baseball and ice cream or in other things?
3. Do you think it's unusual for a boy to have so many adult friends?
4. Who do you think invited the reporter, Henry Leeds, to Ali's birthday party?
5. Why was a reporter invited?
6. What is the purpose of a newsletter?

USING YOUR ENGLISH

REPORTED SPEECH

A. As you learned in Unit 48, when you report what somebody said, you frequently change the tenses of the verbs used by putting them, when possible, one tense farther back in time.

Original Statement or Question	Reported Speech
Present Tense ⟶	Past Tense
Past Tense Present Perfect Tense } ⟶	Past Perfect Tense
can/may/will ⟶	could/might/would

Changes in pronouns depend on the meaning and on who is talking to whom.

The sentences below repeat parts of Bill's conversation with Laura. Say what the original words were and decide who said them.

Example: I asked if you had found a job yet.
   Bill's original words were: *Have you found a job yet?*

1. I told Paulo that you had resigned. _____ original words were:

2. I told him that you were looking for a new position. _____ original words were:

3. He said that he remembered you. _____ original words were:

4. He said that he was looking for a secretary. _____ original words were:

5. He said he didn't think he could hire you. _____ original words were:

6. He said he might be able to find you a job in another department. _____ original words were:

7. You said that you had been doing a lot of thinking.
   _____ original words were:
8. Nora asked me to pick up a few things on my way home.
   _____ original words were:
9. She was saying just last night that she had never enjoyed a job more. _____ original words were:
10. Someone told me that he had heard that they needed another tour guide. _____ original words were:

B. Sometimes you can use either the past or the present tense.

> **Examples:** 1. Columbus said **that the world was/is round.**
> (The idea is true now, as well as when Columbus said it.)
>
> 2. Nora was saying **that she had/has never enjoyed a job more.**
> (She said it recently, and it's still true.)

In the following sentences, decide if the tense of the verb is correct. If it's correct, leave it as is. If it isn't, change it.

1. Copernicus said the earth **revolves** around the sun.
2. Miguel said in his recent letter that he **is having** trouble getting used to Colombia again.
3. He also said he **missed** Marta.
4. Laura has been asking herself whether she **needs** a change.
5. In his speech, Paulo said he **will** not **have been able** to come to any decision about the paintings.
6. Months ago, Pedro told Michael he **hasn't seen** Marian for years.
7. The newsletter said that Ali's birthday **is** wonderful.
8. Mrs. Crawford said that she **had** two children.
9. Michael's friend said that Gary **has** a child.

LESSON 2

Position Available

881   The World's Fair, *Inc. is seeking a bilingual (*Span.-Eng.) tour guide, male or female, to conduct visitors through the major exhibition halls *& pavilions.$_{881}$
882   This individual should be energetic, enthusiastic, & enjoy
883   meeting & working with new people.$_{882}$ In addition, the
884   applicant must be mature, tactful, & poised.$_{883}$ Above all, a tour guide must be self-reliant & able to think on *his/her feet.$_{884}$
885   Tour guides must be in excellent health & be fluently
886   bilingual.$_{885}$ Applicants who have had previous experience in group management are preferred.$_{886}$
887   The salary is $200 *per *wk. including full benefits and vacation.$_{887}$

Please submit all inquiries, together with résumés and letters of reference, to:

888   Ms. Lucille Greene, *Asst. *Dir., Personnel$_{888}$
889   World's Fair, Inc.$_{889}$
890   *P.O. Box 1549-WFP$_{890}$
Flushing, Queens, N.Y.

*Common Abbreviations
Inc. = Incorporated
Eng. = English
Span. = Spanish
& = and
/ = or

per = each
wk. = week
Asst. = Assistant
Dir. = Director
P.O. = Post Office
N.Y. = New York

Questions about "Position Available"

Fact:
The answers are *clear* in the *ad.
1. Is the World's Fair advertising for a male or a female tour guide?
2. Do they want someone to conduct tours in the Spanish Pavilion?
3. What are some of the qualities that they are looking for in a tour guide?
4. Must the applicant speak only Spanish fluently or both Spanish and English fluently?
5. Does the ad say that the applicant must have had previous experience in group management?
6. What does the weekly salary include?

Inference:
You can *guess the right answers* from the ad.
1. Could Pedro apply for this job?
2. Must the applicant be able to make quick decisions?
3. If two otherwise equally qualified bilingual persons applied for the job, which one would get it—the one who had experience in group management or the one who didn't?
4. Is this an easy or a strenuous job?
5. Why isn't this a job for a shy person?
6. Is a résumé the same as a letter of reference?

To the Student:
There are *no wrong answers* to these questions.
1. Do you think Laura would enjoy this job if she got it?
2. What are the advantages of this kind of job?
3. What are the disadvantages of this kind of job?
4. Who would you ask for a letter of reference if you were applying for a job—a business or a personal acquaintance?
5. If you were Laura, would you ask Mr. Crawford for a letter of recommendation?
6. What information do people usually include on a résumé?

*ad is a short form for "advertisement." A *Position Available* ad is also called a "want ad" or a "help wanted ad."

I. Laura is trying to write a letter in reply to the "position available" advertisement. So far, she has written two of them. Which one should she send in? Can you think of anything that she has neglected to include?

A.

1017-32 Maple Street
Whiterock, N.Y.
January 3, 19—

Ms. Lucille Greene
Assistant Director, Personnel
World's Fair, Inc.
P.O. Box 1549-WFP
Flushing, Queens

Dear Ms. Greene:

I am interested in the tour guide position at the World's Fair. I have enclosed my résumé and two letters of reference.

Although my qualifications are outlined in the résumé, I would like to say that I am particularly interested in this job. I have been looking for something interesting and unusual, and this job sounds like what I had hoped to find. I enjoy meeting people, and I get along well with almost everyone.

I am excited about the possibility of beginning something new and look forward to hearing from you soon.

Sincerely,

Laura Segura

Laura Segura

B.

1017-32 Maple Street
Whiterock, N.Y.
January 3, 19—

Ms. Lucille Greene
Assistant Director, Personnel
World's Fair, Inc.
P.O. Box 1549-WFP
Flushing, Queens

Dear Ms. Greene:

In response to your advertisement in The World's Fair Newsletter, I enclose a copy of my résumé.

I have lived most of my life in Mexico and am fluent in Spanish and English. As you will see from the attached résumé, I have been working as an executive secretary in an advertising agency for the last few years, and therefore have managerial experience. The aspect of my last job that I most enjoyed was contact with the clients, and I would be very enthusiastic about a job that required meeting and working with people.

I am available for an interview and look forward to hearing from you.

Sincerely yours,

Laura Segura

Laura Segura

II. Here is an example of a résumé format. If you have read all six
books of *New English 900*, fill it out with information about
Laura. If not, make up the information that you think would best
qualify you to get the tour guide job.

Name:

Address:

Phone:

Date of Birth:

Employment:

Education:

Languages:

Outside Interests:

Related Skills:

References:

LESSON 3

A Letter from London

Dear Michael,

891   I'm sure you thought you'd never hear from me again.₈₉₁
892   But, quite by chance, I read of your triumph in the
893·   newspapers here.₈₉₂ For an instant I wished that things had
happened differently and that I could have been there to
witness my brother's victory.₈₉₃ I'm glad you made it.

894   I am not going to apologize for leaving as I did.₈₉₄ And,
895   knowing you, you probably wouldn't ask me to.₈₉₅
896   Nevertheless, I wanted you to know that I think about
897   you.₈₉₆ I hope one day we can sit down together and talk
about all those things that were on our minds, but remained
unspoken.₈₉₇

898   In the meantime, I would like to ask you to do me one
899   favor.₈₉₈ Tell Mother I am married, that she is a
grandmother, and that for the first time in many years, I am
happy.₈₉₉

900   As you see, there is no return address on this letter, but I
will write again, sooner.₉₀₀

Your brother,

Gary

Questions about "A Letter from London"

Fact:
The answers are *clear* in the letter.
1. How did Gary find out that Michael had won the competition?
2. How does Gary feel about Michael's triumph?
3. Does Gary think Michael expects an apology from him for leaving the way he did?
4. Does Gary hope that he and Michael can talk about the past, or would he rather not discuss it?
5. Had Gary been unhappy for a long time?
6. Can Michael answer Gary's letter or not?

Inference:
You can *guess the right answers* from the letter.
1. Will Michael be surprised to get this letter or not?
2. Had Gary been thinking about Michael, or had he forgotten about him until he read of Michael's success in the newspapers?
3. Does Gary feel sorry about cutting himself off from his family or not?
4. Why doesn't Gary ask Michael to give a message to both of their parents?
5. Does Gary have a wife and child?
6. Why didn't Gary put a return address on the letter?

To the Student:
There are *no wrong answers* to these questions.
1. Do you think Michael's triumph was a good excuse for Gary to write to his brother?
2. Do you think Gary will write to Michael again?
3. How do you think Mrs. Crawford will feel when Michael gives her Gary's message?
4. Do you think Mrs. Crawford will tell her husband Gary's news or not?
5. Do you think Gary and his father will ever reach an understanding?
6. Why do you think Gary wrote the line " . . . for the first time in many years, I am happy"?

"CONTRARY-TO-FACT" CLAUSES

A. The sentences below describe conditions that are not true.

>   **Examples:** I wish *I hadn't eaten dinner last night.* (But I did.)
>   I wish *I had more room for ice cream.* (But I don't.)
>   I wish *I could have come to your party.* (But I couldn't.)

These UNREAL wishes or conditions are sometimes confusing because although the *form* of the verb *looks like* a past or perfect tense, it isn't. It's a subjunctive.

In the following sentences, label the italicized clauses "REAL" or "UNREAL."

1. Yesterday, at the restaurant, I wasn't hungry because *I had eaten an ice cream cone before dinner.*   *REAL*
2. I wish *I had eaten it after dinner, instead.*   *UNREAL*
3. *If I had eaten it afterwards,* I would have enjoyed the dinner more.   _____
4. I wish *I knew the answer to that question,* but I don't.   _____
5. *If I knew it,* I would tell you.   _____
6. *You knew* Michael was going to win the contest, didn't you?   _____
7. *I knew,* even before it happened.   _____
8. *Michael hadn't seen* Leo's painting before he submitted his own, had he?   _____
9. *If he had seen it,* he might have gotten too discouraged to finish his own picture.   _____
10. I wish *I had seen both paintings.* They must have been beautiful.   _____
11. *Paulo could have found out that Michael* was entering the competition under another name. He was in a position to find out.   _____
12. *Leo could have won* if Michael hadn't entered. His painting was excellent.   _____
13. I wish *I could've entered,* because I'd like to study in Brazil.   _____

14. Miguel wished he *hadn't had to leave* New York.

15. *If he hadn't had to leave,* he would be seeing Marta every day..

16. *He probably had never been in love* before he met Marta.

17. Michael wishes *Pedro were more serious and didn't flirt so much.*

18. *If Pedro didn't flirt so much,* he might be happier.

19. *He didn't flirt so much* when he was seven.

20. When I got home last night, I thought *I had lost my keys.*

21. Fortunately, they were in my pocket all the time. *I had forgotten where I had put them.*

22. I would've been in trouble if *I had really lost them.*

B. As you can see, *wish* signals a clause about something; *if* often does, too.

In *unreal* expressions, the form of the verb does not indicate the actual time of the action.

For example:

WISH	REALITY
had been	(but) . . . wasn't/weren't
hadn't been	(but) . . . was/were
had __ed	(but) . . . didn't
hadn't __ed	(but) . . . did
could have __ed	(but) . . . couldn't
couldn't have __ed	(but) . . . could
could __	(but) . . . can't
couldn't __ ⟶	(but) . . . can
were/was	(but) . . . am/is/are not
weren't/wasn't	(but) . . . am/is/are
____ ed	(but) . . . don't/doesn't
didn't __	(but) . . . do/does
would __	(but) . . . won't
wouldn't __	(but) . . . will

In the sentences below, fill in the blanks with the appropriate auxiliary verb to express reality.

Examples: 1. Ali wishes he hadn't eaten dinner last night, but he
* *did* eat of course. His mother made him!

2. Hussein wishes he had known about the Ice Cream Parlor for his birthday, but he *didn't* know about it then.

1. Bill, Jr. wishes he could have come to Ali's birthday party, but he _____ come.
2. I have often wished that I could fly, but I _____, of course.

*This form of the past tense ["he did eat"] is used for contrast and emphasis.

3. I wish you hadn't told me the bad news when you
   _____.

4. Ali wishes every day were his birthday, but it _____,
   naturally.

5. You wouldn't like it if I teased you about your work, so I
   _____.

6. I would come if I could, but I _____. I just don't have
   time this week.

7. Michael and Pedro wish they hadn't quarreled over Marian,
   but they can't change the fact that they _____.

8. If Michael had been sure he would win the contest, he
   wouldn't have gotten so nervous. But of course, he
   _____ sure until it happened.

9. If Joana hadn't encouraged him, Michael might've given up.
   Fortunately, she _____ encourage him.

10. If I were Joana, I would probably marry Michael. But of
    course, I _____ Joana.

11. If Joana had known Michael would win, she could've
    married him in Book 2 without worrying about 88th Street!
    But she _____ know, so she couldn't avoid the
    worry.

12. The Crawfords wish Gary would come home soon, but he
    probably _____.

C. Follow the pattern below when talking about the hypothetical result of an unreal condition.

UNREAL CONDITION	RESULT
If . . . had _____ed, could have	. . . would have _____ed. might could
If . . . _____ed, were/was could _____ would _____	. . . would_____. could might

Fill in the verbs in the following sentences. Sometimes only one will make sense. Sometimes several different ones are possible. In these cases choose the meaning you want.

Examples: 1. If you *ate/slept* better, you *would* be healthier.

2. If you *could/would* turn down the radio, I *might/could/would* get some sleep.

3. If I *could have* helped you with the homework, I *would have*, but I couldn't possibly. I didn't understand it myself.

1. If Paulo _____ found out about Michael's assumed name, he _____n't _____ told Joana.
2. If Paulo _____ been one of the judges, he _____ n't _____ come to any decision at all.
3. If Pedro _____ find a girl like Marta, he _____ be a lucky man.
4. Joana doesn't know what she _____ done if the judges _____n't chosen Michael's painting.

5. Michael _____ come later if he _____ known there were going to be a lot of speeches.
6. If Miguel _____ what Pedro knows, he _____ be cynical, like Pedro.
7. If that _____ my picture, I _____ be proud of it.
8. How _____ you like it if somebody teased you about your work?
9. If Michael _____n't won, he _____ had to go into business with his father.
10. I don't think he _____ done that, though, even if he _____ lost.
11. I _____ gone to work yesterday if I _____, but I couldn't get my car started.
12. If only I _____ more time to practice, I _____ speak English fluently.
13. If English spelling _____ regular, it _____ be a lot easier.
14. Gary _____ not _____ left home if his father _____ been more understanding.
15. If wishes _____ horses, beggars _____ ride.

NEW ENGLISH 900

THE INTONATION LINES

The next ten pages contain the 150 Base Sentences found in this book. They are arranged by unit. The sentences are not accompanied by the context in which they appear in the actual lessons.

The blue lines that appear with a sentence indicate how it is spoken in American English. If you look at the lines you will be able to recognize the basic intonation patterns of English. The language employs three pitches: low, medium, and high.

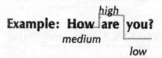

Example: *high* **How are you?** *medium* *low*

The intonation lines should not be used independently, but should be studied along with the sentences as they are spoken, either by your teacher or on the tapes that accompany the book. It is not really possible to learn how to produce a sound by studying only a printed representation of that sound. As you repeat the sentences aloud after your teacher or after the tapes, you will gradually become familiar with the intonation patterns and learn how to use them.

751 You'll come down at Christmas.

752 Everything will be taken care of.

753 They say that fares are going to be reduced in the next six months.

754 The time will pass quickly.

755 I might even be able to come back to New York next summer.

756 Your mother will find you a nice girl, you'll get married, and live happily ever after.

757 All I know is that you are going to be taken away from me.

758 I'll write every day, whether you answer me or not.

759 Look, here come Mrs. Ortega and Pedro.

760 I hope we're not interrupting anything.

761 Let me give you a kiss, my boy.

762 Remember me to your mother and father.

763 I hope to see them again.

764 You'd better hurry, Miguel.

765 Only passengers are allowed beyond this point.

766 We don't know him very well, and he might be too busy to come.

767 I understand his store is being renovated next week.

768 He's been invited.

769 I'm sure he'll try his best.

770 The invitation can be sent out first thing in the morning.

771 I'm going outside.

772 Don't be too long.

773 I thought he might have gone to the Fair.

774 I've looked all over.

775 He should have been back an hour ago.

776 He could have had an accident.

777 Yes, he could have, Zahra, but he probably didn't.

778 I must have.

779 I suppose I should have called you earlier.

780 He must have gone to Mr. Yamamoto's.

781 Why didn't you tell me where you were going?

782 Mr. Yamamoto, I can't thank you enough for bringing him back.

783 It takes too long to invite people by mail.

784 I started walking, and then I didn't know where I was.

785 So I asked people to help me find Mr. Yamamoto's store.

786 Some people said, "Turn left," and some people said, "Turn right," and sometimes I forgot what they said.

787 Anyway, all of a sudden, I was right there in front of Mr. Yamamoto's store.

788 It was like magic!

789 You should have seen him, Mrs. Nikzad.

790 When Ali found the store, he may have been shaking a little, but he wouldn't cry.

791 I've been back over a week now.

792 I expected to have trouble adjusting to life in New York, but no one ever told me that I would have trouble readjusting to my old life!

793 I get angry at things that never used to get me angry.

794 And unless I calm down, I'm going to lose my friends, too.

795 I must have changed.

796 I miss Marta every minute, but I won't say any more about that because I can just hear you making fun of me.

797 Which reminds me, how did your interview go?

798 Did you get the assistant manager position?

799 I know you don't write letters, but you could send a postcard every now and then.

800 I must have been in a daze when I left New York.

801 Attention young artists!

802 The winner will receive a $10,000 a year grant to live and study for two years at the institution of his choice anywhere in Brazil.

803 All men and women under thirty years of age are cordially invited to enter.

804 During December we will be exhibiting as many entries as possible at the World's Fair Museum of Modern Art.

805 But, as the judges, all internationally famous artists, must make their decision before January 1, the Brazilian Pavilion must receive your entry by December 1.

806 On January 1, the Brazilian Pavilion will have the pleasure of announcing the results of the competition.

807   The ceremony will take place in the Grand Gallery of the Museum at 4:30 p.m.

808   All works of art remain your property and will be returned after the first of the year.

809   As we cannot be liable for paintings submitted to us, please insure your entry against loss, damage, or destruction.

810   Persons related to the staff of the Brazilian Pavilion are not eligible to enter the competition.

811   Happy Birthday, Ali.

812   What should I wish for?

813   You know, Mr. O'Neill, by the time we left the house, Ali had asked for ice cream at least half a dozen times.

814   I'm glad I didn't let him have any.

815   I hadn't expected such a big turnout.

816   A reporter for *The World's Fair Newsletter*.

817   I wish I hadn't eaten dinner last night.

818   I hope you don't get sick.

819   But even if I do, I won't be sorry.

820   I wish I had known about this place for *my* birthday.

821 I wonder if it's a giant ice cream sandwich!

822 I wish it were my birthday every day!

823 I'm glad it's not.

824 I wish I could have come to your party.

825 I wish we had invited everybody in the world!

826 Sure, but van der Zee is a fine painter, and he's much better known than I.

827 So what?

828 But I wish I knew if I was wasting my time.

829 If you knew what the future was going to be like, life would be boring.

830 I didn't know that you had become a philosopher.

831 And I had forgotten that you could be such a pain in the neck.

832 Let's change the subject.

833 If he knew what I know . . .

834 He'd be cynical, old, and unhappy, like you.

835 If you could find a girl like Marta, you'd be a lucky man.

836 By the way, why are you so dressed up today?

837 It couldn't be just for the unveiling of my painting.

838 In a nine to five job!

839 I never thought I'd live to see the day.

840 Hey, give me a break!

841 I asked if you had found a job yet.

842 I told him that you had resigned.

843 And that you were looking for a new position.

844 He said that he remembered you.

845 What else did he say?

846 He said he was looking for a secretary.

847 But he also said he didn't think he could hire you.

848 Because he does a lot of work with Mr. Crawford's office.

849 He said he might be able to find you a job in another department.

850 That reminds me, she asked me to pick up a few things on the way home.

851 Yes, she was saying just last night that she had never enjoyed a job more.

852 You said that you had been doing a lot of thinking.

853 Yes. I was thinking that maybe I needed a change.

854 Have you ever thought about being a tour guide?

855 Someone told me that he had heard that they needed another Spanish-English tour guide.

856 I would be proud to say that I had done it.

857 But even if he had found out. he certainly wouldn't have told me.

858 Ladies and gentlemen...

859 Why doesn't he get on with it?

860 If I had known there were going to be a lot of speeches, I would have come later.

861 The judges, as you can imagine, had a very difficult time choosing a winner.

862 Say something like, "Most of the paintings were garbage."

863 And if I had been one of the judges, I don't think I could have come to any decision at all; but, fortunately...

864 I need some fresh air.

865 The judges are making up their minds.

866 You can say that again.   867 Have a bite.

868 But whatever his name, there can be no doubt that he is a master.

869 The world can expect great things from his brush.

870 I don't know what I would have done if Paulo had said some other name.

871 A guy is seven only once, and Ali Nikzad made the most of it.

872 What is closer to a boy's heart than ice cream and baseball?

873 And so, at Ali's birthday party there was plenty of ice cream and lots of baseball equipment.

874 Ali, the son of Mr. Simon Nikzad, a vice president of the International Bank, has always loved the Fair and spends all his free time here.

875 Ali told this reporter that he'd been dreaming of his birthday for weeks.

876 Had his birthday been everything he could have hoped for?

877 Had he been given everything his heart desired?

878 One of Ali's best friends, Mr. Bill O'Neill, an ice cream vendor here at the Fair, was at the big party.

879 So was Mr. Kenji Yamamoto, whose well-known vegetable market is near the Fair.

880 When I asked Ali about this, he said, "I don't know anything about girls yet, but I am going to learn about them this year."

881 The World's Fair, Inc. is seeking a bilingual (Span.-Eng.) tour guide, male or female, to conduct visitors through the major exhibition halls & pavilions.

882 This individual should be energetic, enthusiastic, & enjoy meeting & working with new people.

883 In addition, the applicant must be mature, tactful, & poised.

884 Above all, a tour guide must be self-reliant & able to think on his/her feet.

885 Tour guides must be in excellent health & be fluently bilingual.

886 Applicants who have had previous experience in group management are preferred.

887 The salary is $200 per wk. including full benefits and vacation.

888 Ms. Lucille Greene, Asst. Dir., Personnel

889   World's Fair, Inc.

890   P.O. Box 1549-WFP

891   I'm sure you thought you'd never hear from me again.

892   But, quite by chance, I read of your triumph in the newspapers here.

893   For an instant I wished that things had happened differently and that I could have been there to witness my brother's victory.

894   I am not going to apologize for leaving as I did.

895   And, knowing you, you probably wouldn't ask me to.

896   Nevertheless, I wanted you to know that I think about you.

897   I hope one day we can sit down together and talk about all those things that were on our minds, but remained unspoken.

898   In the meantime, I would like to ask you to do me a favor.

899   Tell Mother I am married, that she is a grandmother, and that for the first time in many years, I am happy.

900   As you see, there is no return address on this letter, but I will write again, sooner.

NEW ENGLISH 900

WORD INDEX

On the following pages you will find a list of the words that appear in this book. They are arranged in alphabetical order. Each word is followed by a sentence.

like   I don't like dinner parties.

This is the sentence in which the word first appears in context in the book. Following the sentence, two numbers are given.

our   Are those students in our class?   3/1

These numbers indicate the unit and lesson in which the word and sentence appear. That is, 5/2 means Unit Five, Lesson Two.

Nouns are listed under the singular form, even if in the book they appeared in the plural.

friend   Where are my friends?

Verbs are listed under the base form.

wait   I'm sorry to keep you waiting.

The only exceptions to the above are irregular forms.

was   I was in the bathroom.

Phrases, idioms, and other units of meaning that consist of more than one word are listed separately.

good morning   Good morning, sir.

This index is not intended to be a substitute for a dictionary, but you will often be able to understand a word from the sentence given with it. You can also refer back to the particular unit and lesson to study the word in a larger context.

children	We don't know him very well, and he might not want to come to a children's party. 44/1
chisel	The world can expect great things from his chisel. 49/2
choice	The winner will receive a $10,000 a year grant to live and study for two years at the institution of his choice anywhere in Brazil. 45/3
Christmas	You'll come down at Christmas. 43/1
classmate	Some of Ali's classmates are being invited, too. 44/1
collector	Artists, critics, collectors, everybody. 49/1
confirm	The reservations haven't been confirmed yet. 44/1
cordially	All men and women under thirty years of age are cordially invited to enter the competition. 45/3
counselor	Have you ever thought of being a counselor? 48/2
count on	I hadn't counted on so many people coming. 46/1
critic	Artists, critics, collectors, everybody. 49/1
damage	As we cannot be liable for paintings submitted to us, please insure your entry against loss, damage, or destruction. 45/3
daze	I must have been in a daze when I left New York. 45/2
definitely	Definitely. 50/1
desire	Had he been given everything his heart desired? 50/1
destruction	As we cannot be liable for paintings submitted to us, please insure your entry against loss, damage, or destruction. 45/3
differently	I know I see the world differently now, but I don't want to be the person I was before I went away. 45/2
discreet	Paulo can be very discreet. 49/1
discussion	Let's not continue this discussion. 47/1
dispense	Why doesn't he dispense with the formalities? 49/1
disturb	I hope we're not disturbing anyone. 43/2
drip	Watch it, your ice cream is dripping. 49/2
Easter	You'll come down at Easter. 43/1
educated	He's much better educated than I. 47/1
effect	Say something original to the effect that, "Most of the paintings are garbage." 49/1
elect	They say Smith is going to be elected. 43/1
eligible	Persons related to the staff of the Brazilian Pavilion are not eligible to enter the competition. 45/3
embarrassed	I would be embarrassed to say that I had spent so much time on the report. 49/1
encourage	He's been encouraged to come. 44/1
energetic	This individual should be energetic, enthusiastic, and enjoy meeting and working with new people. 50/2

enthusiastic	This individual should be energetic, enthusiastic, and enjoy meeting and working with new people. 50/2
entry·	But, as the judges, all internationally famous artists, must make their decision before January 1, the Brazilian Pavilion must receive your entry by December 1. 45/3
equipment	And so, at Ali's birthday party there was plenty of ice cream and lots of baseball equipment. 50/1
exhibit	During December we will be exhibiting as many entries as possible at the World's Fair Museum of Modern Art. 45/3
experienced	He's much more experienced than I. 47/1
explore	He is an independent guy and insists on exploring the world by himself. 50/1
feelings	Even if I hurt her feelings, I won't be sorry. 46/2
flash	There is a flash from the camera. 46/1
fly	The weeks will fly by quickly. 43/1
formality	Why doesn't he dispense with the formalities? 49/1
full-time	In a full-time job! 47/2
gallery	The ceremony will take place in the Grand Gallery of the Museum at 4:30 p.m. 45/3
garbage	Say something like, "Most of the paintings were garbage." 49/1
gentlemen	Ladies and gentlemen… 49/1
giant	I wonder if it's a giant ice cream sandwich! 46/2
grand	The ceremony will take place in the Grand Gallery of the Museum at 4:30 p.m. 45/3
grandparent	I wish my grandparents hadn't died before I was born, but they did. 46/2
group	Applicants who have had previous experience in group management are preferred. 50/2
guide	Have you ever thought about being a tour guide? 48/2
guru	I didn't know you had become a guru. 47/1
hit	Ali almost got hit by a car. 44/2
honor	I would be honored to say that I had been a part of the project. 49/1
idealistic	If he knew what I know, he wouldn't be so idealistic. 47/2
immigrate	I might even immigrate to the United States. 43/1
in addition	In addition, the applicant must be mature, tactful, and poised. 50/2
increase	They say the company is going to increase our salaries. 43/1

reduce They say the airlines are going to reduce the fares. 43/1

register I hope he has already registered for classes. 46/2

related Persons related to the staff of the Brazilian Pavilion are not eligible to enter the competition. 45/3

reluctant I would be reluctant to say that I had worked for Mr. Crawford. 49/1

remind Which reminds me, how did your interview go? 45/2

renovate I understand his store is being renovated next week. 44/1

repay You know, Pedro, there is no way I can repay the kindness that you and your family have shown me. 45/2

reply He may not reply to our invitation. 44/1

reporter A reporter for *The World's Fair Newsletter*. 46/1

resign I told him that you had resigned. 48/1

resolution I might not make any New Year's resolutions this year. 43/1

responsibility Nora was saying just last night that she has handled so much responsibility. 48/2

result On January 1 the Brazilian Pavilion will have the pleasure of announcing the results of the competition. 45/3

résumé Please submit all inquiries, together with résumés and letters of reference, to: Ms. Lucille Greene, Asst. 50/2

return All works of art remain your property and will be returned after the first of the year. 45/3
  I hope to return one day. 43/2

right Anyway, all of a sudden, I was right there in front of Mr. Yamamoto's store. 45/1

right away Paulo said, "*I need* someone right away. 48/1

roller skates I wonder if it's a pair of roller skates! 46/2

rush If he knew what I know, he wouldn't rush into marriage. 47/2

sage I didn't know you had become a sage. 47/1

salary They say our salaries will be increased. 43/1

scenery I need a change of scenery. 49/1

search I've searched high and low. 44/2

seat belt You'd better not unfasten your seat belt. 43/2

security Only passengers are allowed through the security check. 43/2

self-confident Nora was saying just last night that she has felt so self-confident. 48/2